SMOKING FOOD AT HOME

SMOKING FOOD AT HOME

Maggie Black

DAVID & CHARLES
Newton Abbot   London   North Pomfret (Vt)

Drawings by Elizabeth Morris

British Library Cataloguing in Publication Data

Black, Maggie
  Smoking food at home.
  1. Smoking of food — Amateur's manuals
  I. Title
  641.4'6   TX609

  ISBN 0–7153–8484–8

Typeset by Photo·Graphics, Honiton, Devon
and printed in Great Britain
by A. Wheaton & Co Ltd, Hennock Road, Exeter
for David & Charles (Publishers) Limited
Brunel House   Newton Abbot   Devon

Published in the United States of America
by David & Charles Inc
North Pomfret   Vermont 05053   USA

Contents

Acknowledgements

My largest debt of gratitude is certainly due to Mrs Kate Walker, without whose guidance and advice this book would never have survived. It has benefited greatly from her scientific knowledge and tested processing techniques.

I should also like to thank, for advice on ventilation and construction materials for smokers, Andrew I. C. Black, MCIBS, and Mrs Maggie Clarke. Mrs Pat Howard advised on certain aspects of smoked foods in the diet.

I have used with confidence and success the range of 'hot-box' smoke-cookers made by Brooks Productions Ltd and the 'kettle' barbecue smokers made by Weber-Stephens Products (UK) Ltd and Living Flair Ltd. Other goods were kindly supplied by Frank Odell Ltd (handling materials, fuels and firelighters), Alcan Ltd (diamond foil), and Bacofoil Ltd (containers for cheese-smoking). McCormicks Foods Ltd supplied all the spices used for testing. John West Foods Ltd provided canned products such as fruits in natural juice. The cheeses used for testing came from the Danish Agricultural Producers, turkey meat and products from the British Turkey Federation.

The jacket picture owes its splendid produce to the generosity of McConnell Salmon Ltd for the fresh salmon and to Pinney's Smokehouses Ltd for the smoked salmon. The expertise of the staff of Presto Foods guided my choice of other fish and supplied the products. Rex Bamber's skill moulded these elements into an artistic whole.

Patient friends tested the recipes, Mrs Pat Knights and Mr and Mrs Jim Heinemann in particular. More patient still, Miss Pauline Kierney, Mrs Judy Stafford and Mrs Adelaine Hain typed many drafts of seemingly unending alterations to the manuscript.

Lastly, the book has gained immeasurably from the contribution of Mrs Elizabeth Morris who drew the pictures.

1
Why Smoke?

Bathing food in smoke is one of man's most ancient ways of handling protein foods to preserve them. Throughout history, it has been both a commercial enterprise and a skilled home craft because many people have had to depend on it for survival.

Now, of course, we do not depend on it at all. Village stores and city supermarkets are crammed with frozen, canned, dried and packeted preserved foods from all over the world, as well as foods smoked commercially for good flavour. In fact, when mechanised preserving techniques, mass production and modern transport made commercially preserved foods available to two-thirds of the world, traditional domestic home smoking almost died out.

Nonetheless the smoking of foods is becoming more and more popular again as a home craft. Its two simple basic techniques have remained almost unchanged essentially since ancient times, but modern equipment and short-cut variations on these old techniques make them practical for anyone to use on a small scale. Both country and town dwellers can get great pleasure out of mastering the traditional skills and producing delicious food products and also find lots of practical advantages in doing so.

For a start, it is a cheap way to live well. Vacuum-packed bacon is expensive, and is mild and moist compared with the old-style country-cured bacon which some of us still remember; but, by smoking at home, a 2lb/1kg piece of meat can be processed just as easily as a whole side. Smoked German sausage is much more expensive than plain raw pork or beef sausages, more costly still than sausage-meat spiced at home. A smoked mackerel fillet is at least twice the price of the same weight of fresh fish. If you smoke the fresh products yourself, you can turn them into luxury ones – and notice that the foods mentioned above are comparatively *cheap* when fresh, not themselves luxury foods. A side of smoked salmon is delicious, but so are smoked fish which you have caught yourself. Cheap supermarket cheese in fact smokes better than a fine mature Cheddar.

Except for rare commodities which you want to serve on a special occasion, it is more rewarding to enjoy any costly foods you get just as they are, and to smoke perishable everyday foods, making them more varied and flavoursome.

The oldest time-honoured smoking method is called cold smoking. Meat, fish or fowl are first salted for some hours or days, and dried off lightly. They are then hung in cool smoke which never rises above a temperature of 90°F/32°C until they are well dried and impregnated with smoke. As practical home economy, cold smoking is most useful for large-sized pieces of meat or quantities of fish. It can be a valuable money-saver as well as a pleasant craft for anyone who goes in for bulk processing for the freezer.

In the second ancient smoking technique, called hot smoking, the raw food, salted and cold smoked first, is then bathed in moderately hot, smoke-laden air which cooks it while giving it extra flavour from the aromatic smoke essences swirling round it.

The modern revival of smoking as a home craft began modestly as a way of speeding up this process. It started in Scandinavia, where anglers wished to process just one or two fish on the

1 Catching and smoking salmon in the sixteenth century (from a contemporary manuscript)

river-bank or seashore for immediate picnic eating. In this short-cut form of hot smoking, which I have called 'hot-box' smoke-cooking, the food is placed in an almost sealed metal box, and is cooked in hot smoke under slight pressure. The average cooking time is no longer than in ordinary cooking – much quicker than the hours or days needed to salt and smoke foods in traditional ways.

Unlike the traditional methods, this and other forms of smoke-cooking (for instance smoke-roasting in a covered barbecue or domestic oven) only marginally improve the keeping quality of the food; so like ordinary cooked food it must be refrigerated if not eaten as soon as it cools. But this short-cut form of hot smoking does provide delicious hot or cold food anytime, independent of any power source. It makes holiday, party and family catering easier and more interesting too. Since the 'hot-box' is portable, it provides a hot meal anywhere – on the beach, at a picnic, or for a summer supper in the garden or back-yard. Once the fixed quantity of fuel is set alight, you can leave the closed smoke-box: when the fuel burns away, the cooking stops automatically. The food can be eaten at once, while still piping hot, but it need not be; picnickers can go rambling and come back hours later – the meal will not be overcooked, only cooled and smokier in flavour, and it will have been safe from flies and other pests in its closed box.

Smoke-cooked foods are also fun. Starting from cheap super-market products, they make party fare which tastes rare and succulent; they're especially good for a barbecue-style party – and can even take over from a barbecue if 'rain stops play'.

Smoke-cooked foods have a different flavour from the fine foods smoked in traditional ways, whether cold smoked or hot smoked – the method varies with the type of food. Centuries of experience have shown that some foods such as smoked salmon are good to eat after cold smoking alone. Other cold-smoked foods like our breakfast bacon or kippers need ordinary cooking before use (without more smoke). Foods which for safety or flavour are generally hot smoked and then eaten cold include trout, eels, mackerel, poultry and game birds, and venison. Some foods can be processed in a variety of ways: herring, for instance, provide cold-smoked bloaters and kippers, and hot-smoked Scandinavian buckling. Some European continental sausages can be bought either cold or hot smoked.

Most people who have travelled in Europe are nowadays much

9

more willing to try the rich variety of traditionally smoked foods available there. Smoking our own foods gives us all the chance to prepare some of these for ourselves, and also to enjoy smoked foods which are too costly to buy even if they can be found in local shops. Perhaps more important, modernised smoking techniques offer us a chance to pursue an old and fascinating craft (developing our own brines and spicing mixtures if we wish), and to offer with pride our own, uniquely delicious craft foods.

NB In all recipes, imperial measures are given first, followed by metric measures. To avoid confusion with British measures, American measures are listed separately *after* the ingredients.

2
The Smoking Processes

The first way of preserving food was to dry it. Hunters of primitive communities must often have seen the carcasses of fish or beasts which had died naturally and been dried by the sun or wind. Perhaps they returned to old camping-grounds and found desiccated remains, charred but still edible, in the ashes of a fire. When they caught or killed more than their small group could consume all at once, it must soon have occurred to them that they might be able to dry the surplus for hungry days.

At first they probably just stuck fish or meat on poles to dry in the air, as people still do in some parts of Africa. The food would be edible if soaked, but while drying its smell was disgusting and pests attacked both meat and men. Carcasses carried back to camp and hung up to dry near the fire, or over it, dried more quickly and were free of maggots; they tasted better too.

When meat was hung over the flames of smouldering wood, drips of juice and fat fell from it into the fire, making it flare and smoke. The meat acquired a different, tangier smoky flavour, even more pleasing.

Salt
Peoples near the sea or a salt supply soon found that it preserved flesh foods just as drying did, and also flavoured them. So dry salt or heavily salted water (brine) was used more and more to 'cure', that is preserve, fish and meat. Ancient peoples did not know it but they had discovered the best preservative we have; if salt really penetrates into a foodstuff, it prevents destructive bacteria growing more effectively than anything else.

Smoke-drying
Primitive peoples found that they still had to dry most foods, even after salting them. Salted wet food became scummy and too salty

11

to eat after a while, even if soaked in fresh water; it was also difficult to store. Food which was thoroughly dried, especially if hung in cool smoke near a smouldering fire, kept indefinitely, and could simply be left hanging up until needed. It was easy to transport, and tasted good when soaked and cooked afterwards – or even in some cases raw.

This way of smoking food almost without heat is now called cold smoking.

Right through history, as long as people were dependent on local food supplies which became scanty or non-existent in winter, or in famine or wars, salted and smoked foods were vital to their survival. Wherever livestock had to be killed off in winter for lack of fodder, the meat which poorer people had until spring was mainly heavily salted and smoked bacon. Even more heavily salted, dried or smoked meat and fish were the permanent diet of seamen on sailing ships and armies on the march. The Roman armies made smoked sausages popular all over Europe because they carried them as rations in their knapsacks.

Then, in later centuries, when the Christian church imposed two or three meatless days a week on everyone under its sway, almost anyone living inland in Europe came to depend on salted or smoked fish, usually herring, to keep his soul safe. Mass starvation was once threatened in Sweden when pirates blockaded her ports and cut off supplies.

Smoke-cooking
Primitive man's fires were seldom hot enough to cook the food hung above them to dry; but as smoking and cooking techniques became more sophisticated, people found that certain foods, such as sausages, were pleasanter to eat if, after cold smoking, they were dried off in *hot* smoke. In effect, they were cooked. Hot smoking, the most important form of smoke-cooking, had arrived.

Slowly, several variations on basic cold-smoking and hot-smoking processes were tried. The most important was to add sugar and other spices to the salt used for preserving, making a pickle. Spices had been known as preservatives since the dawn of history, when the ancient Egyptians used them for mummifying their dead; but rubbing spices into meat joints before smoking, or adding them to the brine (salt and water) used for curing, came later. A minute quantity of saltpetre in the brine, for instance, was

12

2 A medieval abbey's kitchen
and smokehouse

found to give cold-smoked meat a rosy colour when it was eventually cooked, as well as helping to preserve it.

Sometimes spices were used on meat or fish without salting it first. Shellfish, for instance, might be pickled in spiced vinegar instead of salt, and lightly cold smoked.

CHANGING NEEDS

Smoking food became a commercial enterprise in early times. In ancient Rome, large municipal smoke-houses supplied fish, meat and sausages for the teeming population. Wealthy Romans had smaller private smoke-houses attached to the kitchens of their villas, while on any country farm, whenever a pig or other beast was killed, parts of the animal would be cured and smoked to feed the household and probably the farm workers. Most country housewives, especially farmers' wives, became skilled at salting, spicing and smoking foods to store against winter or war, or just to avoid waste.

Their old craft ways of smoking remained unchanged for about 1,800 years. Up and down England, even in the heart of London, there are eighteenth- and nineteenth-century smoke-houses or 'ovens' still being used by craftsmen-butchers and fish-processors. The great aristocratic households had almost disappeared by 1850, and their huddled domestic offices, the dairy, butchery, smoke-houses and the rest, had been swept away. But even in the late nineteenth century there were still many country farmhouses with wide kitchen fireplaces and chimneys where brined hams and bacon sides were hung to smoke.

However, as so many thousands of people, both rich and poor, moved into town quarters, only the very wealthy still had to feed a large household of servants or estate workers on bulk standby foods. By the late nineteenth century, too, local and home-preserved foods were no longer vital winter fare. Factories were churning out mass-produced foods, improved roads and transport moved them quickly anywhere and soon refrigeration meant that fresh meat and fish could be imported from overseas in cold storage, bought, and stored at home still frozen until needed. The old-style home crafts of curing and smoking meat and fish were, like the craft of baking bread, no longer necessary.

However, people still *wanted* the familiar traditional cured and

smoked foods. Bacon and hams, pickled tongues, smoked sausages, and in Britain smoked herrings such as kippers and bloaters,
were not displaced by the new preserved foods. They were simply
taken over as manufactures, first by local small factories, then by
huge mass-production plants, at home and abroad. Bacon, especially, became a mass British import.

There were good reasons for this. Pickling and smoking take up
space; most modern kitchens are too small for the old-style
processing, and anyway most of us neither want nor have the cash
to store preserved flesh foods in bulk; it is more convenient to buy
a vacuum-pack of bacon when we want one. And since factories
took over the old craft, animals have been slaughtered under controlled conditions, and fish and meat are inspected rigorously for
cleanliness; today's products are 'safe', which wasn't always true.

The trouble is that the mass-produced foods are now barely
flavoured, so that they offend no one's taste, and impersonal
without a hint of local individuality; and some are expensive.

MODERN COMMERCIAL PROCESSES

In large-scale commercial production, bacon, hams and many
other foods are now salted 'instantly' by injecting brine into them;
and the components of smoke are often added in the form of
flavoured paint or as powder to minced mixtures, or by infra-red
and electronic processes which 'smoke' a ham in ten minutes.
Speeding up the processes makes them cheaper as well as producing standardised mildly flavoured products which the supermarket
customer anywhere knows will vary little.

Food preparation with brine pump and needle, and the use of
smoke powders, are feasible at home too; but even if you have free
supplies of the raw foods you cannot compete costwise with the
commercially produced products when using these methods, and
they do not resemble the craft skills in brining and controlling
smoke that produce fine personal products. Doing it the old way –
or rather in today's version of the old way – offers more than this:
the satisfaction of creating a brine just right for a particular food,
of learning by experiment how long a particular product needs in
its salt bed or bath, and the triumph of offering golden-tanned,
glossy, generously flavoured foods that stand comparison with
renowned gourmet delicatessen fare and cost much less.

MODERN AIDS TO USE

'Doing it the old way' need not mean following in detail all the more laborious (and sometimes inefficient and unsafe) processes used in the past. It would be foolish not to make use of modern materials and appliances, such as a heavy-gauge metal smoke-box or, for some purposes, a domestic oven, or commercially prepared wood-dust or chunks. The wide choice of prepared herbs and spices in packets or jars allows you to flavour smoked foods in countless ways today without the hassle that spicing and salting involved in the past. Even making a salt 'bed' or brine used to be hard work, because kitchen salt usually had to be scraped off a block and crushed by hand. As for spicing, the only way to do it besides making a flavoured brine was to haul down the hams or bacon sides (or other meat) from their hooks once or twice daily while smoking them, rub them with hand-ground spices or hand-chopped herbs and rehang them for the next bout of smoking. Since cold smoking could take up to a fortnight, brawny arms were needed for all the hauling and rubbing of the weighty joints.

In the past, too, the fire for smoking had to be re-lit daily, and watched constantly to make sure that it smouldered evenly, neither bursting into flame nor settling to sullen embers. If the kindling and boughs were still green, they might not light properly; if resinous softwoods were included by mistake, the bacon on which a family might depend all winter could be ruined in an hour by billowing acrid smoke; even someone leaving the kitchen door open might be enough to set up a draught that oversmoked the precious meats.

Today the various grades of salt and the spices we can buy are quick and easy to use. We can vary the fuel and the temperature we use at will. The volume of smoke in any smoking chamber can be controlled fairly accurately, once we have decided how much we want. The next chapter therefore looks at home smoking's one vital constituent – the smoke itself.

3
How Smoke Works

Although both cold and hot smoking were first developed to help preserve flesh foods, neither in itself can do so for very long. What the smoke really does is secure the keeping-quality of food that is at least partly preserved by other means. We also use it to give foods a unique delicious flavour and colour.

Food can be preserved in four ways. The bacteria which poison it or make it decay live in moisture, such as meat or fruit juices, and breed most rapidly when the juices are warm, fresh and sweet. Poison-forming and decay-breeding bacteria die or are dormant in completely dry food or in food saturated with salt. Nor can they operate in acids or alcohol, or in foods heavy with certain chemicals such as aldehydes.

Bacteria are also dormant without air and in temperatures below freezing-point. Most are actually destroyed by heat above boiling-point, and some by quite low heat; this is why most of our milk is pasteurised.

Smoke, directly or indirectly, assists in creating conditions in which bacteria cannot flourish.

WHAT SMOKE IS

Smoke consists of warm air carrying a 'mist' of minute specks of various chemical compounds and other substances formed by burning wood. The main ones that help to preserve and flavour food are aldehydes, ketones, phenols and acetic acid, together with alcohols, resins and waxes.

DRYING: WHAT SMOKE DOES

Even 'cold' smoke is slightly warm, so it tends to rise. This draught of warm moving air very slowly dries food exposed to it. Foods are usually hung up for cold smoking, so the smoky air circulates freely all round them, and all their surfaces and crannies are exposed to the drying effect of the draught as well as to the chemicals in the smoke. Chemicals in the smoke which actually penetrate the food may also help to coagulate its juices and 'set' its fibres.

In hot smoking, heat dries and stiffens the previously cold-smoked food still more.

In smoke-cooking, the drying effect of hot smoke seals the surface of raw food almost at once, as pre-cooking does, so smoke never penetrates the food to any extent. So this kind of smoking has virtually no preservative effect, although it gives the food a delicious flavour and rich surface colour.

THE GERM-KILLERS

Certain chemicals in smoke help to kill off bacteria on the surface of food and inside it. They also help to inhibit the growth of new bacteria, although they do not prevent it. Phenols, aldehydes and acetic acid are all germicides, along with resins and waxes; during smoking, rising warm air deposits these on the surface of the food, and in cold smoking some seep into it. Those which stay on the surface kill off surface moulds; those which penetrate dissolve in the liquid remaining in the food, and kill or check the growth of yeasts and some other bacteria.

Another effect of phenols in smoke is to help keep animal fats fresh-tasting. Fat on the cut or skinned surface of butcher's meat, poultry or game tends to combine with oxygen in air, and then turns rancid. The phenols act as anti-oxidants.

In cool Atlantic climates, fresh foods which have been correctly handled before and after slaughter, and which have been properly brined and smoked or fully cooked, seldom contain dangerously harmful bacteria. However, a few of the most dangerous bacteria are highly heat and smoke resistant, and in areas where they flourish, special precautions must be taken: see page 170.

SMOKE FLAVOURS, AROMA AND COLOUR

The chemical components of smoke are the agents which flavour food, as well as helping to preserve it. Many people claim that

18

smoke from particular types of wood gives food a special aroma and flavour. The smoke from resinous softwoods certainly does, but the flavour is usually unpleasantly bitter. Chestnut and juniper, however, are attractively aromatic woods which, if used as the only fuel, do seem to give foods their own faint but distinctive taste and scent. Apple, cherry and a few other fruitwoods are said to do so, but the flavour is generally so subtle that only a trained palate can detect it, and food with a strong flavour of its own will overcome the wood-smoke's contribution. The smoked product tastes, to most people, just the same as food smoked over the standard hardwoods, oak or hickory, which are generally used.

Any standard hardwood fuel can be given a more distinctive scent if it is sprinkled with dried herbs such as juniper, rosemary or bay leaves while it burns. Although it is doubtful whether they actually give any flavour, the lingering scent which clings to the food when smoke-cooking is pleasant. Packaged 'burning herb' mixtures sold for barbecuing can be used for a stronger scent.

Most cold-smoked foods, and certainly hot-smoked ones, become a deep golden, chestnut or peachy colour all over, and the inside flesh is also darkened or tinted. Smoke-cooked foods do not get smoke-tinted all through, since the food's surface is sealed by the heat and the smoke gets no chance to soak right into it; the surface colour may vary from a deep chestnut to a pale gold, and it may be patchy.

In foods smoke-cooked in a hot-box there may sometimes be a risk of staining, especially if the roof or lid of the smoking chamber or compartment is dirty: the heat can make wet foods give off steam, which condenses on the 'ceiling' of the container, combines with any smoke resins there, and may then drip down on the food, or be shaken on to it when the box lid is removed. To prevent this happening, dry food thoroughly before smoking, or film its surface with oil.

It is worthwhile making sure that smoke-cooked food looks as good as properly cold-smoked or hot-smoked food, even if you resort to tricks – for instance, slipping the food under the grill for a few moments to gild it. Since our eyes dictate to our appetites, beautifully tanned food satisfies us more than patchy or pallid products, even if commonsense says that the colour is simply the result of smoke resins mingling with the thin film of grease on the food, or its surface moisture.

4
Making Smoke

When certain materials, such as wood, are heated or touched by a flame, they burn or smoulder, provided they have enough air. The more slowly they burn and the less heat they create the better, from the food-smoker's point of view. What you want is a fuel that burns or smoulders steadily without needing much care or creating any more heat than is needed for cold smoking. It must also create clean sweet-smelling smoke which does not give food a bitter flavour or leave crude tarry deposits on it. Many fuels are not suitable; in fact the choice of really good ones is surprisingly small.

GOOD FUELS TO USE

Wood, and in some places peat or such dry materials as maize cobs (corncobs), have been the traditional fuels used for food smoking. Wood, by far the most common, is still used by nearly all amateur craft food-smokers. It is easy to get, adaptable and has proved the best. It ignites easily, burns slowly and gives off minimal heat, when correctly controlled.

Not all kinds of wood, however: there are some you must avoid. The resinous woods of conifers such as cedar and pine smell superb when they burn, but the effect of their aromatic smoke on food is quite different: it contains bitter tarry particles which flavour food unpleasantly and may also be harmful. Also they burn fast and tend to flare. So although such softwoods are easily cut and easy to set alight, they should be banned from the smoking site. Some people include softwood twigs or chips when building the fire, just to get it going, or add a proportion of softwood to hardwood dust towards the end of the smoking time, because it gives the food a deep glowing colour; but this is unwise, because any stock of softwood bits or dust could easily get mixed with the hardwood fuel being used. Stick to hardwoods!

Hardwoods

Almost all hardwoods burn well and slowly, and give a sweet, reasonably mild smoke. English oak and hickory are the best-known traditional smoking woods, but ash, beech and many others are also good. Some people have firm favourites and equally distinct dislikes, sometimes without good reason. Juniper belongs to the same family as the cypresses and is highly scented, so it sounds dangerously like a softwood – yet it is a popular smoking wood in Italy and elsewhere.

The fruitwoods, such as apple and cherry, are common favourites, but the problem lies in obtaining them: orchard owners do not regularly fell their trees, so even fruitwood enthusiasts have to use other woods sometimes. (If you want to experiment with scented smoke, you can buy packets of wood-burning herbs and spices.)

If you are inexperienced in choosing fuels, play safe. Do not, for example, accept wood chips, shavings or sawdust from the local sawmill without finding out what kinds of wood are included.

The form in which you use your chosen fuel depends on what kind of smoking place you have, and the kind of smoking you intend to do. Suggestions are given in the directions for each main smoking method. For serious regular smoking, sawdust is the most reliable fuel; it smoulders easily without flaring, and is easy to top up. It is the only fuel used in hot-box smoking.

Whatever form of wood you use as your main fuel, it must be dry though not bone-dry. Dustbowl-dry fuel is needed only for igniting the fire; after that it burns too fast. Green wood, still sappy from the tree, is sometimes recommended for ad-hoc smoking, but it is difficult to light and behaves unpredictably, tending to produce volumes of smoke when you least expect or want it. The wood must be compact, not crumbling, and clean; smouldering rotten wood smells decayed and foul.

Sources of fuel

For occasional smoking for fun, you will probably be able to get fuel without much trouble. You may have some hardwood logs intended for the grate that can be sawn up or chopped. For regular craft smoking you will need a more substantial consistent supply, at fixed intervals, of both fire-making and smoking fuel, say sawdust, shavings and chips. One common source is likely to be a

21

local sawmill or timber-yard, provided you make sure that you are not being sold assorted woods which include softwoods. Ask if you can have a regular consignment of a single specified kind of wood such as oak (or hickory in the USA). There are often other sources around: a boat-builder's yard, a furniture factory, even a local craft centre or do-it-yourself store.

Most manufacturers of commercial electric-powered smokers and hot-box smokers sell sawdust in bags for use with the appliance. It is a costly way of buying fuel for a large kiln, but can be a useful standby while you arrange a regular supply.

MAKING THE SMOKE

There's no smoke without fire – or rather heat. The smoke-producing fuel for your smoking chamber has to be ignited and kept smouldering at the level that gives the quantity of smoke you want, at the right heat.

There are various ways of supplying the heat. The simplest, and the traditional way, is to make a hardwood fire, putting the smoking fuel on top of a bed of glowing hardwood twigs, chips and chunks. For slower burning, a traditional alternative to woods is a charcoal fire, with hardwood chips, shavings or sawdust scattered on top. You can build it with barbecuing lumps or briquettes.

Let the fire, whether of wood or charcoal, burn down until it has a really hot heart before adding the smoke-producing fuel. Any aromatic wood sprigs or leaves, such as bay or rosemary, should only be added when smoking is well under way.

Though much craft smoking is still done with a wood or charcoal fire, a modern smoking chamber can also be treated by a gas burner or a poker run on butane gas, or by a similar electric element if the smoking equipment is near a power supply. When heated by gas or electricity, the smoking fuel is placed on a shallow fireproof tray, a fuel-carrier, which is supported above the heating element, so that the effect is the same as when sawdust is heated (without the tray) on top of charcoal. In small-scale hot-box smoking the fuel is usually heated by pans of methylated spirit set alight under the steel box holding the hardwood-dust smoking fuel and the food. For lighting the pans and for lighting a wood or charcoal fire, use tapers. And do not forget the other vital element for making smoke – the matches.

Starting a fire

The old-fashioned country way was to push a redhot horseshoe into a pile of sawdust in the smoker. It could easily be hooked out and reheated. Nowadays the more certain way is to crumple a ball of newspaper with one or two standard barbecue firelighters broken into pieces; alternatively use granules or jellied alcohol. Impregnated 'instant-lighting' charcoal briquettes can be used to get a charcoal fire going, but never soak charcoal in methylated spirit or any other liquid fuel.

A portable gas poker or small blow-torch would get your fire going without trouble, or simply use a wax taper – which will save you scorched fingers and a lot of matches on a windy day outdoors.

In any smoker with an upper and lower part to the smoke compartment, as in the dual-purpose masonry smoker shown on page 30, starting the fire presents no problems. A gas-ring or burner, or an electric element, in the lower part soon makes the steel plate above it very hot and ignites any fuel placed on it – with steady heat that encourages the fuel to smoulder, not flare into flame.

As for any form of gas or electric heating, all that is needed is to make sure there is enough gas in the cylinder, or that you have a properly earthed working electricity supply.

Keeping it going

Keeping a fire going is usually just a matter of topping-up the fuel and giving the fire enough air to keep it smouldering steadily. The air vents with their dampers and/or baffle-plates installed in any permanent smoker (page 33) should ensure that the fire can get the air required to keep burning at the slow, steady level you want. However, every smoker seems to develop a personality of its own, and reacts well or grumpily to certain conditions, no matter how well it is designed and built; a wood-fuelled smoker may refuse to heat to the level you want for hot smoking when the wind is in a certain quarter, so that you have to open bottom dampers more than usual, or remove baffle-plates in a trench. Only experiment will show you how to deal with your smoker's particular quirks.

Although the chances of a simple home-made smoker or impromptu smoker misbehaving are greater, it may well be easier to deal with. In most such smokers, you can get at the fire fairly easily, and an air-pump or stout pair of old-fashioned bellows, or even the strength of a good pair of lungs, may save your smoking day and your dinner.

This does *not* apply to a hot-box smoker. Never apply a blast of air to any liquid fuel – in fact don't let a draught near it. If smoking outdoors, see that you have a means of making a windbreak. If the methylated spirit under the smoke-box refuses to light, or goes out when lit, put up the windbreak or turn the smoker round to protect the access to the pans from draughts, and try again.

If you use a gas ring or burner, especially in a home-made smoker, watch that the jet-holes do not get clogged by falling ash, or even by charred scraps or drips from the food. A thin poultry skewer may be needed to clear them.

5
Getting Started on Smoking

Your smoking-place can be as large as a shed or as small as a suitcase: it depends on what kind of food you want to smoke, and how much of it, and also on your available space and money. You can smoke a lot of herrings in the space taken by two sides of salmon. If funds allow, you may opt for a professionally built brick or block structure to use regularly; or you may decide just to build an impromptu smoker when you give a party or catch more fish than the family will eat all at once. Or you can buy a ready-made portable smoke-cooker.

If you think you will take up smoking seriously as a craft or hobby, the first decision needed is how much you will spend to get started. Chapter 10 describes the basic gear needed, and by getting your local prices for the various items you can work out the basic cost of the kind of smoking you wish to do; then you can add further items if you wish.

THE KILN OR SMOKER

Food which is just hung over a camp-fire is unlikely to get properly or safely smoked. Rain, gusts of wind or drips of fat which make the fire flare are obvious hazards. Unless you are going to bake, grill or fry it on the spot, food must first be well salted, then bathed in cool moving smoke for long enough to make it safe to eat raw, or must be smoked with extra heat until it is fully cooked through. This means that you must smoke it in an enclosed space where you can control the smoke supply.

Craft food-smokers talk about their smoke-house, kiln or smoke-oven. They tend to use the terms interchangeably, but by a smoke-house they usually mean a freestanding permanent building normally used for cold smoking and at least as large as a garden shed. By a kiln or smoke-oven they may mean a structure the size

25

of a small room or a little cabinet the size of a rabbit-hutch. What is generally called a food-smoking 'kiln', however, is fairly large and permanently sited, and can be used both for cold smoking and the hot smoking that follows it when required.

A smoke-oven is used in the same way as a kiln but is usually smaller. It may be a permanent structure, for instance part of a brick barbecue, or an improvised one such as a converted dustbin (garbage can). It may be built to last, or be a temporary affair of loose bricks put together for one day's use. The term 'smoke-*box*' is sometimes used to describe the smaller box-shaped ones, but misleadingly so, because manufacturers have cornered that term to describe the portable steel boxes designed for the modern smoke-cooking technique I call 'hot-box' smoking.

The term 'smoke-oven' covers most home-smoking structures; but since we all associate the word 'oven' with the use of fairly high heat and cooking, it may be unhelpful. Therefore the general label 'smoker' is used here for almost all smoking places and smoke-containers that can be set up and used at home by the hobbyist, although I shall sometimes use 'kiln' if referring to a larger smoking-place. The terms 'smoke-box' or 'hot-box' are used here just for commercially made smoke-cookers.

To be practical as a modern hobby, if you are going to smoke food more than just now and again, your home smoker should be able to supply 'cold' smoke and also, with extra heat, to give hot smoke for hot smoking and perhaps for smoke-cooking. So here we describe the essential features of home kilns suitable for both cold and hot smoking. We look at some of the types you can make, and the other equipment you need.

PERMANENT OR PORTABLE?

The biggest item, even if you build it yourself, is the actual smoker; its cost can vary from a few pounds (or dollars) to hundreds. If you intend to take up food smoking seriously and do it regularly, you need a permanently sited kiln or smoker of some kind; something you have to set up and dismantle every time you set to work will not do. Apart from the time and nuisance involved, you would only be able to smoke a limited range of foods, and in small quantities. You would therefore find it difficult to develop safe smoking techniques and create top-quality products. You also need a smoker whose behaviour you can predict no matter what technique or variation you use, and no matter what the weather.

However, if you want to smoke foods mainly as a social activity, or because your interests lie outdoors and you want a means of making quick outdoor meals, then a portable smoke-cooker is for you (page 58). There are all sorts of ways in which you can use a hot-box – for instance, from making smoke-cooked hot dogs as fund-raisers at a club function to processing some of your own catch on site if you enjoy fishing.

Permanent or portable? The choice is yours. If in doubt, play safe: try using a portable smoke-cooker for two or three months and see how you get on. You may find yourself wanting to go on to more serious, bulk smoking, or you may find the portable apparatus gives you all you want.

Choosing a portable smoke-cooker involves much less serious decision-making than building a permanent structure, but it still needs some care. If you will smoke-cook mainly for parties, there is a lot to be said for a kettle-style smoke-cooker which can be wheeled to the site, provided you have a smooth path without steps. On the other hand, if you will smoke-cook mainly for quick meals at picnics or when camping or fishing, a hot-box which you can put in the car is better. Pages 58–67 describe the kinds of portable smoke-cooker available, and how and where they are best used.

6
Building a Permanent Smoker

For home food-smoking, a permanent smoker means a purpose-built brick, concrete or steel structure, on permanent foundations, and not movable. It includes commercially made smokers dependent on mains electricity – but not a few old bricks slapped together on a couple of paving stones.

If you want to build a permanent kiln or smoker, the first essential is to find a suitable site. You can adapt an outhouse, stone or brick shed or barn, or build in the open. For this you need a flat open space that can be stripped of bushes or trees without ruining the surroundings. There must be room for a rubbish pit or bin where you can hygienically dispose of scraps of food, empty tins or other garbage, for a fuel store if possible and for a fire pit and trench if that is the heating system you wish to use. The site should also be near a power supply and your kitchen if you wish to do any smoking-plus-cooking that involves using the oven. Even if you plan to do only cold smoking, stay close to base; you will not fancy trudging a long way with a trolley-load of food to smoke, and repeating the trip every time you wish to inspect the smoking rate.

This may mean settling for a medium-sized or fairly small smoker near the house; but you will want it to be screened from everyday view, unless it is to be built as part of your garden or patio design. This can cost a bit more – a basic smoker is simply an uncompromising block or pyramid with a hole at the top. As the hole emits smoke when in use, it is best placed downwind from the house and any garden feature such as sitting areas, swimming pool or tennis court; and from any neighbouring ones too! It should have its back to the prevailing wind.

Having found a good site the next step in Britain is to get any building permission required from your local authority. Find out if you need a permit. You may have to submit plans of the proposed

28

structure; if so, you have to decide now exactly what you are going to do. It may be a nuisance at this early stage of your planning, but do not ignore this step. Local authorities can be strict and may even make you pull down something they did not approve.

Before you draw up your plans, make sure that the proposed smoker will not contravene any clean-air regulations, such as Britain's 1955 Clean Air Act and its later amendments. Check, too, whether having a smoker near your home or in an unused room or outbuilding will involve you in taking out extra insurance cover. Should you think of selling your smoked food, remember that some landlords do not let their tenants carry on a business on the property or take up activities which could annoy neighbours, and that there are similar restrictions in the deeds of some owner-occupied houses.

In any case, before you start building a substantial permanent smoker, check with your neighbours that they understand what you intend to do and agree to it. Get that agreement in writing to forestall any later problems. You may love the smell of wood smoke drifting from the smoker on the evening air, but if your neighbour's washing, garden plants or windows get filmed with smuts and smoke when the wind blows in his direction, he is likely to have different views. If you want peace and quiet, you will be wise to take his reactions into account.

Having established that you will neither be taken to court nor drummed out of the neighbourhood, there is nothing to stop you building your permanent smoker. Read this chapter carefully, and talk to local experts if you can, to make sure you choose the right smoker design: then go ahead.

PLANNING A MASONRY SMOKER

Before you embark on building any masonry smoker, whether of bricks, blocks or slabs, draw a plan of it even if you haven't already had to get one made professionally for the planning authority. Draw a proper scale-plan that makes clear the size, shape and position of every part of the smoker and what it is made of.

The illustrations in this book are intended as guides, not exact plans. Note the various essential features of a smoker below, and make sure that they are all included. List the materials you intend to use – firebricks or a concrete mat for the base of the fire

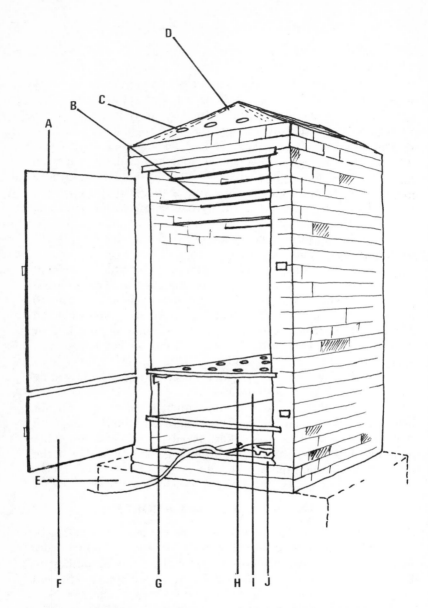

3 Simple dual-purpose masonry smoker (type 1). A, upper door; B, three sets of rods; C, smoke escape holes; D, peaked roof; E, foundation below ground; F, lower door; G, flange supporting base baffle-plate; H, baffle-plate; I, upper part of fuel and fire compartment; J, lower part

30

compartment, for instance – and their cost. Make sure that all materials are available.

Shape

The most practical shape is a square-based squat pillar, taller than it is wide, to make the most economical use of the smoke (drawing 3). The smoke rises and is diffused evenly, the smoker's considerable weight is distributed evenly on its foundations, and the square base is easy to set against a wall or to build into a barbecue complex. Remember that the smoker front must be at least 22in (560mm) wide so that the door can be wide enough for loading and unloading the food.

You could build a cylindrical smoker, like a British pillar-box, but it would not fit in easily with existing straight walls, and some space would be wasted inside because the curved door again must be wide enough for loading and unloading.

Size

The smoker can be any size you like over 24in (610mm) square. But for economy, a smoking chamber 6ft 6in (1.98m) high and 3ft (910mm) square is a good practical size. It is not too expensive to heat, and is easy to reach into, but holds a good quantity of food.

Features

A smoke-house may be a similar structure to a chimney, or like a shed with a chimney compartment attached (see drawing 13). A smaller smoker's interior usually consists of a large upper chamber where the food is smoked (placed on hooks or racks), and a smaller fire compartment below to hold one or both heat sources and often the fuel too. The division between the two compartments can be fixed or removable, but in a small-scale smoker a movable one is more practical. Preferably, it should fit closely inside the walls of the smoker, and have holes in it to let the smoke through; this gives better smoke distribution than the alternative of a solid plate with gaps between the sides of the plate and the smoker walls. In a small smoker, it can also be supported securely on flanges projecting from the walls of the smoker.

If you buy a commercially built, electrical smoker (see drawing 4), the fuel is best placed in removable drawers or boxes, which

31

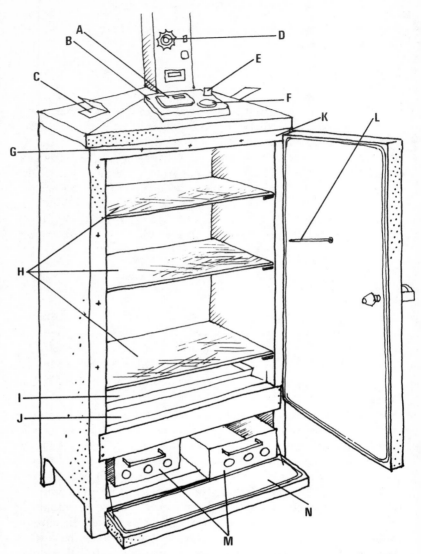

4 Commercially made electric smoker. A, pilot light; B, 13-amp supply fuse; C, air louvre; D, smoke-outlet damper; E, temperature controller; F, on-off switch; G, sensor tube for temperature controller; H, removable shelves; I, drip-tray; J, electric elements below expanded metal base (hidden); K, 5 horizontal rods below roof for hanging food; L, dial thermometer on door; M, fuel drawers; N, fuel compartment door

can be slid in and out through an opening at the bottom; the opening is sealed by the front of the drawer when smoking is in progress.

Your smoker must always have some kind of an opening through which you can get access to the fuel and fire, and which you can seal partly or wholly to control the quantity of air entering the smoker. See below.

The roof of the smoker may be pitched or flat, but it too must either have a central opening acting as a chimney, or a number of small holes through which the smoke can escape. The circulation and escape of smoke is easier to control if you have a number of small holes arranged in a rectangular or circular grid pattern, the latter being easier to construct for a pitched roof. Remember that you need to make shutters or flaps, ie dampers, to cover the holes so that you can close them when required. If you make a central hole, it should have a chimney pot, to raise the outlet above the level of a flat roof or the ridge of a pitched one.

Materials
Steel or the more costly cast iron are the only safe metals to use for a furnace or oven. Like most metals commercially available, steel is prone to corrosion which may be accelerated by temperature and humidity; and apart from this, it heats up considerably if standing in hot sunshine – your cold smoker could become, in effect, a natural hot smoker! For these reasons, metal should not be used for the main body or roof of a permanent smoker standing in the open air. If you decide to use metal to build a permanent smoker under cover, say inside a disused stone or brick outhouse, remember that your design must allow for the expansion of the metal under heat.

Concrete or breeze blocks, or bricks, are suitable for the body of an outdoor smoker, but the fire compartment must be fully lined with fire-bricks or other non-combustible material. A valuable new material worth investigating is a very light ceramic fibre which insulates the walls of the fire and smoking compartments, and saves wastage of heat and therefore of fuel.

Take care to line the floor of the smoker. Building a permanent smoker on bare ground is not wise. For one thing, any masonry smoker needs solid foundations, and digging them will churn up the earth so that it is difficult to flatten evenly. The floor will inevitably get dirty, and with cleaning its level will gradually sink; then it will have to be covered anyway, with a lot more trouble than doing it at first.

Any weatherproof, heatproof material in which holes can be made if required can be used for the roof.

A material such as galvanised sheet steel can be used for the doors of a small smoker or for flaps over vent-holes. Drop-down or sliding latches are best for easy handling when hot (see drawing 6).

SMOKER LAYOUT

In a dual-purpose small kiln or smoker, that is one to be used for both cold and hot smoking, a first consideration is where the burning fuel is to be placed. It has to fill the smoking chamber with as much cool or hot smoke as is wanted, for as long as you want it, but no longer; so you must be able to get at the smouldering fuel and its heat source during smoking, to remove ash or to top up the fuel, or to increase the draught of air that makes it burn.

As smoke rises, being warm air, the heat source must be put at the bottom if it is inside the smoker, well below the food to be smoked; the fuel is then placed on top of it. Do not, however, put the heat source on the floor of the chamber itself: you may not be able to reach it during smoking without opening up the whole smoker (or going right in, if it is a large kiln), interrupting the smoking process and suffering smoke-filled eyes and lungs.

Instead, put the heat source, whether hardwood, charcoal, a gas burner or an electric heating element, in a removable fireproof container, or a tray with a rim deep enough to confine a living fire if needed; in other words, in a 'firebox'. Add the smoke-producing fuel to a live fire, or put it on a flat fireproof tray (a fuel carrier) firmly placed over a gas or electrical appliance.

You need a closable opening in the smoker wall through which the firebox can be put into the smoking chamber and removed when necessary. As smoke and heat spread out as they rise, the firebox can be quite small. In a large kiln or smoker you can use two or three flat-bottomed fireboxes, and slide them one by one through the door, or put them where wanted in a walk-in kiln. Besides letting you deal with the fuel and heat easily whenever you want to, having a removable firebox or boxes will make cleaning the kiln or smoker floor much easier.

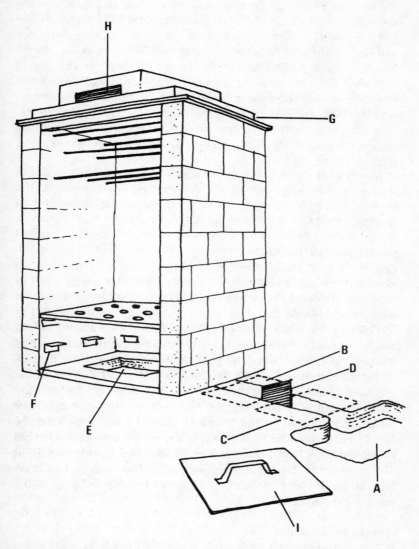

5 Simple dual-purpose masonry smoker (type 2). A, fire-pit; B, inlet to
smoker; C, removable metal sheets covering trench; D, baffle-plate (slate,
tile, etc) slotted into trench; E, smoke outlet; F, flanges for supporting
solid plate; G, flat roof with chimney; H, damper or baffle in chimney; I,
fire-pit cover

For cold smoking, an easy way to control the quantity and temperature of the smoke is to place the heat source outside the smoker itself. A fire is made in a pit some distance from the smoker, at the end of a covered trench which carries the smoke into the smoker. The longer the trench, the cooler the smoke (drawing 5). This is quite a good, simple way to control the smoking process, because you can get at the fuel at any moment, just by lifting the cover off the pit or off any part of the trench. You can also control the quantity of smoke flowing along the trench by inserting baffles, such as slates, part-way across it at intervals along its length and at the inlet to the smoker.

If you want to use a fire or small stove above ground as a heat source, a drainpipe can be used to carry the smoke instead of a trench; but it is much less easy to open up for inspection or inserting baffles.

Letting the fuel 'breathe'
Smouldering fuel or a fire must have air to keep it alight. If possible this air should reach it through an inlet which you can close, partly or wholly, when the fuel burns too fast or when you have finished smoking.

The air inlet, which must be below the fuel or on a level with it, can be created in various ways. A fire in a pit can be laid on a bed of craggy pebbles which don't pack down closely together; breezes or bellows stimulate smoke production and direct its flow to the smoking chamber. Then, when required, natural air currents are blocked simply by covering the pit. A brick structure can have air-holes left between the bricks at ground level, which can be blocked to reduce the air flow, while a steel one may have a hinged side-opening or flap-down fire-door (drawing 6). If wide enough, it can 'double' as the opening through which you can pull or hook out the firebox or fuel carrier without disturbing the food in the smoking chamber.

A second heat source
It is important to have a second source of heat, especially when you use a remote heat source as your main one; it cannot supply enough heat by itself for hot smoking or any kind of smoke-cooking.

A second source of heat may also be a useful back-up in an

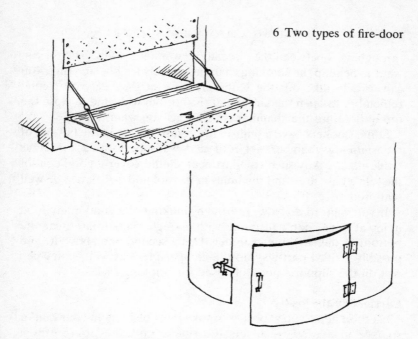

emergency. If sudden rain soaks the fuel in a pit halfway through smoking, you need not then abandon the process and risk the half-smoked food becoming bacteria-laden as it cools.

Diffusing the smoke
For safe smoking and flavoursome products the smoke must swirl all round the food, bathing the whole surface and getting into every nook and cranny. If it lingers, however, it will give the food a bitter tarry flavour. To let the smoke escape, there must be an outlet at the top of the kiln or smoker which you can close when you want to, for instance while heating the chamber to hot-smoking temperature.

If the smoke from the smouldering fuel is left to do as it likes, it will go straight upward in a narrow column and escape through the top outlet, bypassing any food items at the sides of the smoking chamber. Its flow must be interrupted so that it can only reach the top outlet by a difficult, devious route. The simplest way to direct the smoke flow in a fairly small chamber is to balance a removable steel or iron baffle-plate, with scattered holes punched in it, some distance above the carrier holding the fuel. The smoke can then only rise through the punched holes in the plate or round its sides, through gaps between the plate and the smoker walls. Then if you want to heat up the smoking chamber quickly for hot smoking, you can usually take out the baffle-plate to let the heat rise freely; remember to open the air inlet at the bottom wide and to close the top outlet until the chamber is as hot as you want it.

Some smokers have a built-in fire compartment at the bottom of the smoking chamber, its roof and walls perforated to act as baffle-plates. Any such compartment should cover a good deal of the kiln's base area and the holes in its roof and walls must be well scattered.

If you want to do slow, thorough smoking of a good many food items at once, don't just stay with a single baffle-plate near the bottom of the smoking chamber. Use a second one above it, and possibly a third part-way up the compartment as well – they can rest on the supports normally used for smoking racks.

Carriers for the food
Most food items you choose to smoke must be hung in your kiln or smoker in a way which lets the smoke circulate around them freely, reaching every part of them. This is important to give a good flavour to the food and is vital if you want to store your products for any length of time. Large or long pieces of food, such as a turkey split lengthways or a whole chicken, are smoked hanging from hooks, or on strings, from a bar. Small tender items such as flounder fillets which might fall apart if hung up are smoked on removable racks; sloppy or meltable items are best smoked in shallow foil containers or on sheets or trays placed on the racks; these 'bits and pieces' include chicken or turkey livers, mussels, clams and oysters, small slabs of cheese, and salt.

In any small or medium-size smoker, the supports for one rack are placed high up, near the roof, so that long food items can hang down from them on hooks. Two, three or four more racks can be placed lower down in the smoker if it is deep enough. If the racks are almost the same length or width as the smoking compartment, they can be supported on flanges projecting from the interior walls. Some more adaptable smokers have two or three pairs of steel rods fixed across the width of the smoking chamber at different heights, like rafters.

The racks themselves should have strong steel rims and either coarse welded mesh or fine mesh (for small items). As for hooks, the number and sizes you need depend on the kinds of food you will smoke. Small ones can easily be home-made from coathanger wire.

If you have a fairly large kiln, or have inherited or bought an old smoke-house, you may need slightly different equipment for holding the food items. A good, not too costly, piece of equipment for any walk-in smoking chamber is a single-tier clothes rail from a dress shop for hanging bulky and heavy items. In small-scale food-smoking a rail can also be useful for hanging up cold-smoked foods to dry or for storing them. A similar useful piece of equipment for holding small food items in the smoker is a three or four-tier standing 'beanstalk' of wire vegetable racks or typist's in-trays (not painted or plastic-covered).

DESIGNS FOR A MEDIUM-SIZE PERMANENT SMOKER

There are really only three basic designs for small-to-medium size smokers for both cold and hot smoking, although the details of any of them can be varied in dozens of ways; they can be made as fancy-looking as you please. The designs really only differ in the type of heat used or the way it is supplied.

A simple basic design for a medium-size masonry smoker suitable for garden or back-yard use is shown in drawing 3. The fire compartment is divided into an upper and a lower part. This lets you choose where to place the main heat source, and the kind of heat you will use. For cold smoking only, place a small wood or charcoal fire, or a gas ring fuelled by bottled gas, in the bottom part of the compartment, with the fuel above it on the solid steel plate. If, however, you want to be able to start off by cold smoking, and go over to hot smoking partway through the food processing, you can build a small fire on the solid plate and scatter the smoking fuel on top; then, when you wish to heat up the smoker, put any kind of second heat source in the bottom part of the compartment. For easy removal of ash, any fire-door in the bottom of the smoker should be flush with the ground (drawing 6).

This type of smoker is practical and can be attractive if you build it into a barbecue complex and make the whole thing a garden feature. A typical one is shown in drawing 7. Build a fairly small smoker in this case; you don't want it to tower above the barbecue. If the barbecue is right beside the smoker, you can cold-smoke

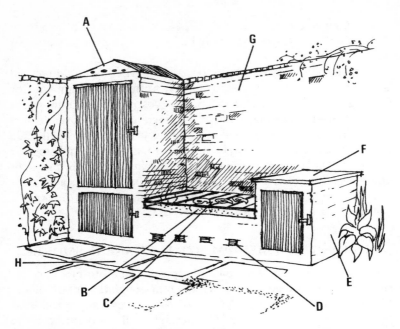

7 Smoker built into barbecue complex. A, smoker; B, barbecue fire; C, barbecue grill; D, air vents for barbecue fire; E, fuel and equipment store; F, worktop; G, garden wall; H, paving

small items and transfer them straight to the barbecue for quick cooking: the food will have an exotically charbroiled-plus-smoke flavour, like some southern European sausages.

The second basic smoker design (drawing 5) differs from the one above in two ways. For cold smoking, its heat source is sited outside it, in a fire-pit below the smoker's level, and the smoke flows, or is driven by a fan or bellows, along a covered trench into the smoker. When it emerges, it is quite cool. The trench need not be lined, provided it is dug in fairly hard ground, but you will need loose overlapping leakproof iron sheets, stones or turfs to cover it, and the fire-pit itself (drawing 8).

To control the smoke flow, you also need baffles to place across the trench at intervals to block it. Use slates, tiles or small pieces of hardwood as deep as the trench and slightly wider. To hold them upright in the trench, blocking it wholly or partly, cut slots in the ground on both sides of the trench and at right angles to it.

40

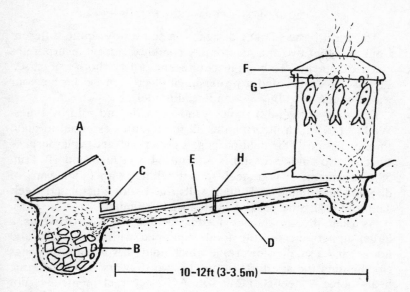

8 Pit heat source and inlet. A, steel cover of fire-pit; B, fire-pit; C, brick covering smoke outlet; D, trench, approx 5in (15cm) wide, 8in (20cm) deep; E, steel sheets covering trench; F, dustbin cover; G, rods and hooks; H, baffle-plate

Make these cuts in two or three places, including right beside the smoker wall.

You'll notice that the fire-compartment has no solid centre plate in this design. If you want to use the smoker for hot smoking, after using cooled smoke from the fire-pit, you can make a fire at the end of the trench *inside* the smoker. Either scatter the smoking fuel on top of the fire, or place it in a suitable fire-box or tray and balance it over the end of the trench.

The smoker in drawing 5 (page 35) has a flat roof, which can be placed on either smoker design. The only problem it sometimes presents is that, if the food is hung near the top of the smoker, the smoke tends to linger around it before escaping. To prevent this, it is worthwhile building a chimney on a masonry smoker, instead of making just a small hole or holes for the smoke's escape. Leave a narrow open slot as wide as the space inside the chimney at roof level when building, and fit a sliding damper into the slot which you can pull out wholly or partly, depending on how much smoke and heat you want to escape.

The third basic smoker design is in some ways quite different from the other two and seems more complex, since it incorporates electric elements. To build it requires the skills of both a practised sheet-steel worker and a professional electrician, so by far your wisest course is to buy a commercial model.

Drawing 4 (page 32) shows a model made and sold by Innes-Walker Ltd which incorporates all the features essential to good smoker design. This dual-purpose smoker (in fact triple-purpose since it also smoke-roasts) is 4ft 5in/134.6cm high and 1ft 11in/58.4cm square. It is a steel-framed cabinet with outer walls of dimpled aluminium and inner walls lined with zinc-plated steel. The roof is slightly peaked, with a small chimney.

As usual, the smoker is divided inside into two compartments: a larger upper one for the food, equipped with both racks and hooks, and a smaller lower one which holds sawdust and shavings (for igniting the sawdust) in one or two drawers. However, one heat source – steel-clad 240 volt AC electric elements – is not under the fuel, as in the other designs, but above it under the expanded metal base of the smoke-cabinet. These black-heat electric elements are thermostatically controlled, the temperature inside the smoke compartment being shown on a dial thermometer on the smoker door.

For cold smoking, no electricity is needed; the sawdust is lit in the ordinary way, and allowed to smoulder black, giving smoke with minimum heat. A damper regulates the amount of smoke in the oven, being kept open for cold smoking to ensure a flow of cool air, and three-quarters closed for hot smoking to allow the temperature to rise. When hot smoking, however, the electric elements are switched on. Being wired in series, they burn with quarter-power so that the heat rises slowly, avoiding any risk of case-hardening the food. The additional heat makes the sawdust burn more quickly, giving extra smoke, which finishes the food with a very good flavour. The control panel at the base of the chimney provides a temperature-control switch to allow selection of the oven heat, which is controlled by the thermocouple in the oven. A pilot light registers whether the power is on or off. The smoker only needs an ordinary 13-amp socket.

The almost foolproof, thermostatically controlled heat of this smoker is ideal if you intend to smoke regularly and reliably; for instance if you get regular supplies of farmed fish, or you intend to cater for a large household or community.

For this kind of handsome smoking machine, you must of course have a suitable home. A disused garden shed or stable can be put to good use, provided you can instal a power supply. Or an old outside larder or apple-store may be just the right size and near enough to the house to make installing the power supply fairly easy.

An outside larder, storeroom or even coal-bunker can often be converted into a simple permanent smoker; for some hints on how to do it, see Chapter 8.

7

Building
a Sturdy Makeshift Smoker

A reasonably sturdy, serviceable, dual-purpose smoker for use in your garden or back-yard can be improvised in various ways. (Portable smokers are described in Chapter 9.)

Visit a hardware store, garage or scrapyard to find one of these: a new galvanised iron dustbin (garbage can); a standard steel oil-drum (barrel); or a disused gas or electric cooker (stove). But check the descriptions below to make sure the one you choose will give you the size and type of smoker you want, and that you can get the other materials, and have the skills, to make it.

Do not try to turn a disused refrigerator into a smoker; its insulation is usually highly inflammable, so it will be short-lived.

DUSTBIN (GARBAGE CAN) SMOKER

A new galvanised iron dustbin will make a smoker suitable for processing small fish, birds and plate-sized pieces of meat (drawing 9). You need 7 steel rods ⅜in (9.5mm) thick and 4in (102mm) longer than the diameter of the bin. You also need a heavy iron tray such as a chef's baking tray to hold the fuel, 4 bricks to support it and 4 larger concrete blocks on which to stand the bin.

The other essentials are a second, slightly smaller, heavy fireproof tray – about 1in (28mm) smaller in diameter than the dustbin (this doubles as a drip-tray and upper baffle-plate (drawing 9); 2 steel mesh racks that just fit inside the bin; heatproof drawer handles or wire to make handles; and any hooks you want to use.

The fuel is generally hardwood shavings and chips set alight by a standard firelighter, or by a butane-gas burner – which also provides extra heat for hot smoking.

With an oxyacetylene torch, sharp cold chisel or hacksaw, cut a fairly large hole in the centre bottom of the bin. The bottom of the

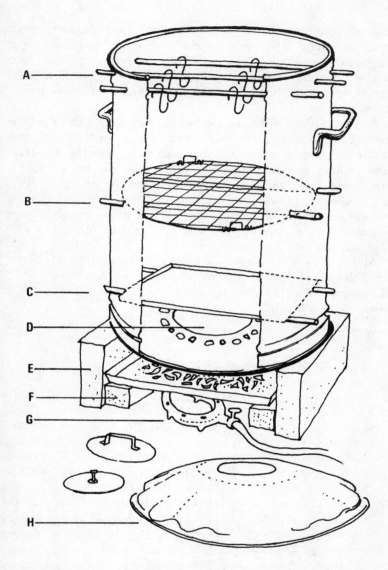

9 Dustbin smoker, showing interior. A, rods and hooks for hanging food; B, steel mesh food rack; C, drip-tray or upper baffle-plate; D, perforated bottom of bin (base baffle-plate); E, concrete blocks on which bin stands; F, bricks on which fuel-tray stands; G, gas-ring, as source of heat; H, dustbin lid, perforated

bin will then serve as the base baffle-plate. Keep the metal piece you cut out to cover part of the hole when cold smoking if required; a projecting screw put through its centre and fixed by a nut will provide a means of shifting it. Make some small holes in the bottom of the bin around the centre one to let smoke trickle through.

Next, cut holes in the sides of the bin through which to put the rods. You will need two rods at an equal height, 4–5in/102–27mm above the bottom of the bin, on which to balance the drip-tray; and another pair of rods about halfway up the bin to hold a steel-mesh rack; and three rods across the top of the smoker, about 4in/102mm below the dustbin lid. These will hold either a second steel-mesh rack or hooks, as you wish. Attach drawer handles or rigid loops of stout wire to both sides of each rack so that you can take them out easily when loaded with food.

Make an escape-hole for the smoke in the dustbin lid; again, keep the piece of metal you cut out so that you can cover part of the hole when hot smoking. If necessary, nick the edge of the lid; it must not fit too tightly.

10 Dustbin smoker in action

Before you use the smoker, season it well, to avoid any metal taint on the first batch of food. You will want to try it out in any case. Stand the bin on stout concrete blocks so that it does not wobble. The blocks should be far enough apart to let you place the fuel tray under the smoker between them, resting on bricks. Put the rods in place, and balance the drip-tray on the bottom pair. Place a small pile of hardwood dust and shavings on the fuel tray, right under the hole in the bottom of the bin; place a gas burner or ring on the ground between the bricks under the fuel. Put on the dustbin lid, with the hole in it left open (drawing 10).

Light the burner, and watch the performance of the smoke when the fuel ignites. It should rise through the centre hole and small holes in the bottom of the bin, then find its way around the edges of the drip-tray and fill the bin. Let it do so thoroughly on this trial run. If possible, top up the fuel, turn down the gas, and let the smoker operate, empty, as a 'cold' smoker for several hours, so that smoke deposits can settle all over its interior.

STEEL OIL-DRUM (BARREL) SMOKER

A steel oil-drum about 3ft/915mm high and 2ft/609mm in diameter can make a good smoker. Smaller steel drums (barrels) can also be used.

Any drum, however, will be difficult to convert if you do not know what it has been used for. The problem is that steel drums are used as standard containers for all sorts of liquids and chemicals, including petrol, and any drum which has once contained petrol is *very dangerous indeed*. You must *not* put *any* form of heat near it even if it seems cleaned and empty; it will cause a serious fire and explosion. Unless you are expert yourself, arrange ahead with a local engineering workshop to clean and strip *any* used empty drum which you acquire, inside and out, before you touch it. Ask for the whole flat top surface of the drum inside the top rim to be cut out in one piece, and have that stripped for you as well. Once this is done, you can start work on the drum yourself (drawing 11).

Cut off the edge of the cut-out top of the drum to make it about 2½in/63mm smaller in diameter than the drum itself. Cut or drill about 16 small holes in the steel to turn the top into a baffle-plate. Next, buy two steel-mesh trays, or three if the drum is a deep one.

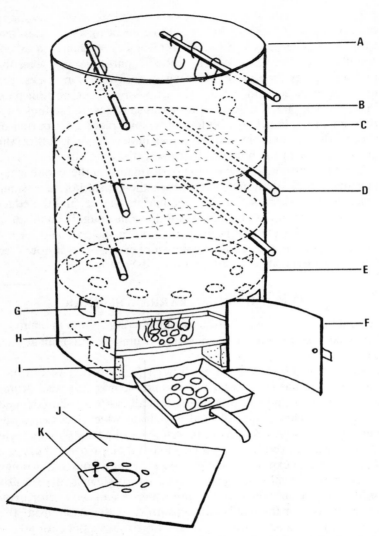

11 Metal drum smoker, showing interior. A, rods across top for hooks to hang on; B, wire handles for steel mesh rack; C, removable mesh rack for small food items; D, rods on which rack rests; E, baffle-plate made from top of drum; F, fire-door cut from side of drum; G, flanges on which baffle-plate rests; H, steel tray holding smoking fuel; I, bricks or blocks on which fuel-tray stands; J, steel sheet cover for drum, with centre hole; K, cover for hole, with screw for lifting off

They will rest on rods or flanges. These carry the small food items and any meltable foods to be smoked in foil trays, so choose a fine mesh. Attach rigid loop-style drawer-handles securely to the edges of both the baffle-plate and your steel-mesh trays. Remember that the trays will be loaded with food when you lift them out of the smoker.

Acquire a steel fire-box or deep tray which will hold a small live fire, and attach to it either a fixed or a hook-on handle. A roasting tin would do, or a rack-holder from under the grill of a small British gas stove (cooker), if not too wide. Cut a rectangular hole in the side of the drum at the very bottom, wide enough to let you slide the fire-box into the drum; it must have no lip at the bottom. Attach hinges and a fastening to the piece of the drum you have cut out, to make a side-fastening fire-door. Attach it to the drum, to cover the space.

Now fit 4 or 6 flanges inside the drum about two-thirds of the way down to hold the baffle-plate. They should be equally spaced apart and at exactly the same height. You can usually buy flat-topped lipped steel handles meant as handles for kitchen drawers which make suitable flanges, provided they project far enough into the drum to hold the baffle-plate securely.

Cut 4 holes in the drum's sides about 4in/102mm below the open top of the drum, in which to insert two parallel level steel rods; these will hold any hooks needed for hanging larger food items. Cut two or three more sets of holes at intervals below the first ones, for rods to support your steel-mesh trays. All the rods should be at least 4in/102mm longer than the diameter of the drum, so that they project on each side, and they should ideally be about ⅜in/9.5mm thick.

The two last fitments you need are a cover for the drum, and a fuel-carrier. The cover can be any piece of clean flat sheet steel which will cover the open top of the drum; drill or punch a pattern of small smoke-escape holes in the centre, and make a flat steel or wooden cover to fit over them, with a projecting screw or similar handle. You can then close some of the smoke-escape holes when necessary, by placing the cover over them.

As for the fuel-carrier, this is just a heavy iron or steel tray; a chef's small flat baking-sheet (tray) is ideal. Support it on bricks or similar blocks under the baffle-plate and above the fire-box. The blocks must be far enough apart for the fire-box to be slid into place between them, and the tray must be far enough below the baffle-plate to get plenty of air through the fire-door.

Add to the collection a gas ring or electric heating element, to use as a second heat source when you want to do hot smoking. You can then make the live fire on the solid fuel-carrier and cap it with smoking fuel, and put the second heat source underneath.

Alternatively, make a fire-pit outside the drum-smoker for cold smoking, and lead the smoke into the drum via a trench; use either a live fire in a fire-box or a bottled-gas appliance as a second source of heat for hot smoking.

COOKER SMOKER

An effective small smoker which stands indoors (eg in a shed) can be made from a disused conventional gas or electric cooker. It is cheap on fuel since it is designed to hold heat, and it is easy to clean. It already has removable metal racks, which can be placed at varying heights to hang hooks from or to hold steel-mesh racks or trays carrying small food items. It also has a full-depth door which makes loading and unloading easy.

A gas cooker is easier to convert than an electric cooker (drawing 12). First remove the burners, then lift off the removable hob and take out the mechanism which feeds the gas to the burners. If the top of the oven slides out, as many do, remove that too; if not, drill 2in/5cm holes in the oven roof immediately below the burner holes in the hob.

To prevent the whole interior of the shed or outhouse being filled with smoke, the holes in the oven top and hob which let it escape must be covered, and the smoke must escape to the outside air through a flue. This will mean making a hole in the shed wall through which you can push one end of a length of non-combustible curved pipe. This pipe should be at least 2in/5cm in diameter, and should have a sliding or butterfly damper inserted in it. The free end should be inserted in a hole drilled in the bottom of an inverted solid steel tray or drawer. This must be large enough to cover all the holes in the surface of the hob; put it over them upside-down, like a canopy. Plug any gaps between the rim of the tray or drawer and the hob with heatproof wadding or sealer.

For cold smoking, you can use either a small live fire in a shallow fire-box as the means of igniting the smoking fuel, or a gas-ring or

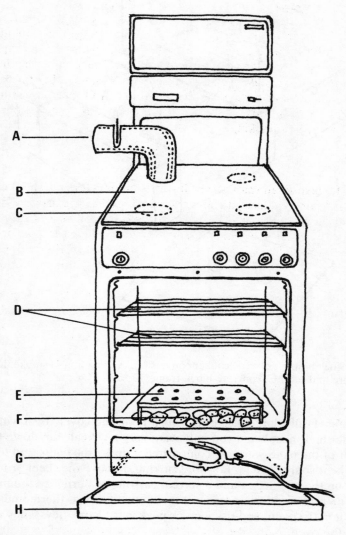

12 Gas cooker converted to smoker. A, flue and damper; B, inverted
steel filing-tray covering holes; C, holes in hob where gas-rings removed;
D, oven racks for hooks or mesh cooking rack; E, foil-covered trivet as
baffle-plate; F, smoking fuel on oven floor; G, gas-ring in plate-warming
compartment; H, drop-down door of plate-warming compartment

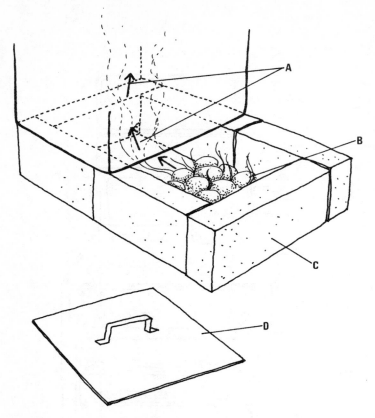

13 Block base for electric cooker conversion. A, direction of smoke flow; B, fire and fuel; C, concrete-block frame; D, cover for fire

burner. Drill some holes in the oven floor and cover them with a loose steel sheet when you only want very low heat. Let down the door of the plate-warming compartment under the oven, and tuck the heat source inside. For hot smoking, remove the sheet or foil, top-up the live fire or add a second gas-ring or burner to the first.

For hot smoking, invest in a good-quality oven thermometer, put it in the oven, and risk a quick peek at it the first few times you use the oven.

An old-fashioned electric cooker is converted in much the same way as a gas one. The rings or hotplates are more difficult to remove, and you may have to cut holes in the top of the hob. A sizeable hole may be needed in the oven floor, too, if there is no plate-warming compartment. In this case raise the oven on a frame of, say, loose concrete blocks extended in front to make an enclosed space: make a fire in the extension topped with fuel in the same way as in a remote fire-pit (drawing 13). Cover the whole extended section with a steel tray or similar 'lid' when smoking, to force the smoke to move sideways and up through the hole into the body of the oven.

8
Shed, Stable or Outhouse Smokers

Almost any small brick or stone outbuilding can be used to house a smoker, or as a smoker itself. A potting-shed, stable or old-style pig-sty, a coal-bunker or an old stone larder leading off the kitchen, as examples, can generally be adapted: but emphatically *not* a garage.

An outhouse smoker often has several advantages. Probably it already fits in with its surroundings. More important, if built of bricks, stone or blocks, it will keep cool in summer. This is a big help, especially if it is large enough to be used as a drying space for brined foods before and after smoking, by building a smaller smoking place inside it for the actual smoking process.

Another advantage of many an outhouse smoker is that you can smoke more varied foods at one time than in other types, and larger quantities, because it is higher; so you can experiment more easily with various techniques. For instance, you can smoke long sausages by hanging them from a shed ceiling, instead of looping them; and try smoking trout high up at roof level and on a low rail near the ground at the same time, to see which taste best.

If an outhouse which seems ideal in other ways is too large in area for the quantities of food you will smoke, this can be overcome – see below. A more annoying problem is likely to be smoke leakage, for instance from between a corrugated-iron roof and cement-block walls. Use mineral-wool wadding to seal such cracks. Seal around the door with flameproof draught-excluder, or by hanging a non-flammable curtain over the whole door inside. Deal with such leaks, however small: wisps of smoke floating away may not seem important but the wastage can be considerable, as well as the nuisance value.

ADAPTING A LARGE SPACE

One obvious way to adapt a shed space which is too large for your usual quantity of food is to build a small home-made copy of a basic permanent smoker inside the outhouse; use part of the outhouse wall for the back of the smoker and use old galvanised iron or steel sheets for the rest of it.

If the outhouse roof is flimsy or has exposed wooden joists or (worse) thatch, put in a non-flammable false ceiling with a good layer of insulating material above it.

When the smoker is built, you can use the rest of the outhouse's interior for drying off foods before or after smoking them. For this, the only adaptation usually needed as a rule is to flyproof the windows, and if possible the door, and to check the walls for chinks and holes to make sure they are pest-proof. It may be wise to paint the outhouse walls inside with a fungicide – certainly in an old stable or pig-sty: famous cheeses are alleged to have been first 'blued' by moulds and yeasts in old stables, but blue ham is *not* what you are after.

A more elaborate way of converting a fairly large stone or concrete-block outhouse, saddle-room or store-room is shown in drawing 14. The outhouse itself is used for drying foods, and for cold smoking. A chimney built on at the back or side is used as the fire-compartment, and is also supplied with racks above the fire for hot smoking. A hole in the outhouse wall, with a damper inserted, conveys smoke into the main outhouse space when it is needed for cold smoking; a second damper in the chimney prevents it escaping by the easier upward route. Brined food hangs from racks or on a dress-rail while it dries, and need not be moved when you want to start smoking; simply make your fire, even before the food is quite ready, and adjust the dampers at the right moment.

The flat roof in the illustration is insulated – to keep the sun's heat out, as much as to hold heat in – and is pierced by one or two subsidiary chimneys to let the cold smoke escape. These, again, have dampers so that the smoke can be held in if needed.

In a stable or piggery, you may be able to build up or cover the walls of one stall or sty to make a small smoker like the plain basic one in the illustration on page 35. To save installing a separate fire compartment (drawing 14), make the fire in a perforated bucket or in a domestic incinerator. As a second heat source, make another

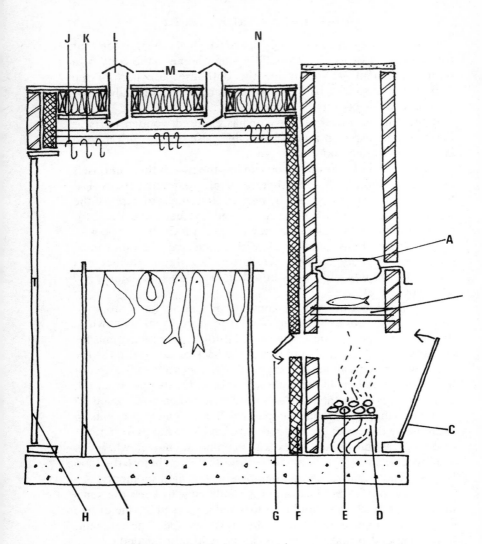

14 Combined smokehouse and storage space with hot-smoking chimney.
A, damper regulating smoke escape through main chimney; B, racks or
rods for hot smoking; C, fire-door leading to 'oven'; D, fire; E, smoking
fuel; F, double or hollow wall between chimney and outhouse; G, damper
regulating smoke entry to outhouse; H, door of outhouse; I, hanging rail
for drying food; J, hooks for cold smoking; K, racks for cold smoking; L,
damper; M, subsidiary chimneys; N, insulation

fire like the first, or slide an ignited gas-ring fuelled by bottled gas into the smoker.

A conventional standard gas or electric cooker should fit neatly into the disused outside 'coal-hole' often built on to the outside wall of an old farm or cottage kitchen. Make sure you have enough room to open the oven door fully.

An old-fashioned outdoor larder or apple-store can be used in the same way.

WOODEN SMOKERS

Don't! Some books on food smoking give descriptions and pictures of wooden structures, from huts to small cupboards. You may read that a dog-kennel or large packing-case can be fitted up as a smoker cheaply and easily. Be wary. Generally a smoker made of wood is hazardous; even when cold smoking there is always some chance of flare-ups. In time, as the wooden walls dry out, planks, shingles or plywood may char or even burn. This can even happen under a fireproof sheathing intended to protect them, and you may not spot the hidden smouldering wood until too late.

Also a wooden structure is difficult to make leak-proof. If much smoke seeps out, as a beginner you will be uncertain how much smoking you have achieved. The nuisance value of the smoke in your own or your neighbour's garden will however, certainly be high.

9
Portable Smoke-cookers

Reliable portable smoke-cookers for use at your home base or when operating from it are of two distinct types. First there are 'hot-boxes' or smoke-boxes. The larger models of the type shown in drawing 15 can be adapted for cold smoking, with the attachment shown in drawing 16, and can if you wish be more or less permanently sited in a suitable outhouse. This type originated in Scandinavia as equipment for amateur freshwater and seashore fishermen, and is made in several sizes. A medium-sized one can be transported in your car or on a bicycle pillion or can be carried knapsack-style and set up on any reasonably flat open piece of ground. The second type are the charcoal smoke-cookers, most of which are like barbecues with hoods and are called 'kettles'; they originated in North America. These are more luxuriously finished than smoke-boxes and are designed mainly for patio or garden use.

SMOKE-BOXES

Smoke-box or hot-box cooking has many merits. As it only deals with thin fillets of food, it can give you a hot meal anywhere within a short time, and without any power supply (even at home, for instance, if there is a power failure or strike). Besides being cheap on fuel, it is ideal for making cheap small food items such as vacuum-packed cheese or ordinary sausages or luncheon meat taste 'different' and good. It is a fine way to deal with extra numbers at a barbecue party or to cope with the foods if a deluge soaks the barbecue (under controlled conditions, the smoking can be done indoors, page 105). It can also preserve that prize trout, small salmon or partridge for at least long enough to let you show it off to your friends before you eat it.

Essentially, any 'hot-box' smoke-cooker consists of a rectangular box (drawing 15(E)), made of sheet steel, which rests on an

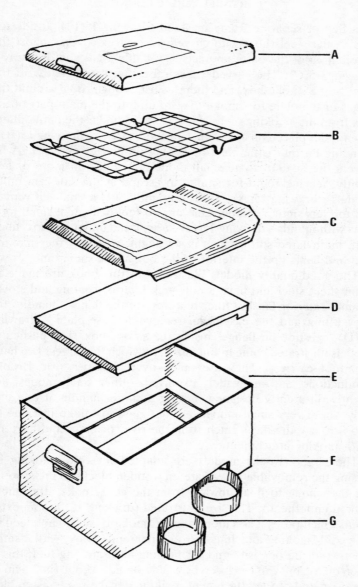

15 Hot-box smoke-cooker. A, lid with vent; B, food-carrier; C, baffle-plate (where foil pans can be placed); D, base-plate; E, smoke compartment with flanges for base-plate; F, fixed frame or stand; G, methylated-spirit cans

attached or separate frame or stand (drawing 15(F)). Inside the box, a flat steel sheet with curved-over edges covers almost the whole area of the base, and acts as a baffle-plate and drip tray – drawing 15(C). The curved edges raise the plate slightly off the base of the smoke-box, and there is just enough room around the edges of the plate for smoke to seep up into the main part of the box from the smoking fuel, which is placed under the baffle-plate. The food is placed on a steel rack or food-carrier – drawing 15(B) – standing on the baffle-plate or resting on flanges above it. A lid covers the box. In some small models, it slides on more or less tightly, leaving room for smoke to escape at the sides; in other models – drawing 15(A) – it fits on tightly, and a small slit vent in the top lets smoke escape. One or two fuel pans, like small food cans without lids – drawing 15(G) – are placed under the box, filled with methylated spirit which is set alight; it ignites the smoking fuel and heats up the interior of the box at the same time.

The good-quality models illustrated in this book are made in 8mm sheet steel and have a non-stick interior coating and stove-enamel exterior finish. Other features are the flanged handles for easy lifting and the easy-clean removable base-plate – drawing 15(D) – resting on flanges inside the smoke-box. The particular models illustrated come in four sizes, of which the largest two have two food-carriers. They are made by the British firm Brooks Productions, and are widely exported. Other small models are slightly differently designed, having a clip-in handle at one end only; these very small models are designed to smoke just one or two fish, say the day's catch from the river or dam, and have no cold-smoking attachment.

The larger Brooks models are adapted for cold smoking by raising the removable base-plate on wooden blocks to make room for the smoke to float upward from the cold-smoke attachment tucked underneath. The size illustrated (drawing 16) has an extra stand which raises it still more; bigger smoke-boxes do not need it. The cold-smoking attachment is an open-ended box, with a small fire-box at the opposite end for heating and smoking fuel; this is open on top but can be closed by a slide-on lid. About 1in/2.5cm of the open end of the attachment is slid under the ready-assembled smoke-box, leaving the open-topped fire-box exposed. The fire is made at this end of the attachment, the smoking fuel is added, and covered with the lid. The rising smoke then has to find its way

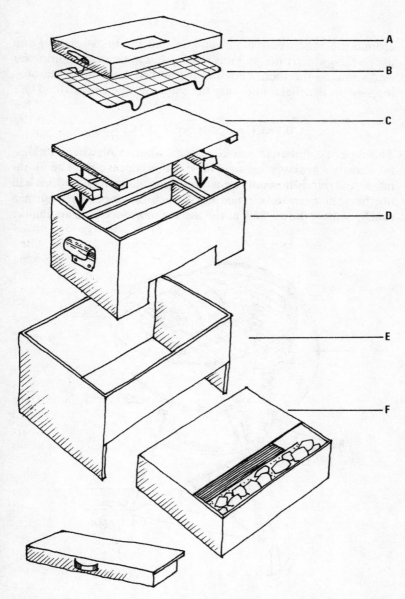

16 Hot-box smoke-cooker with cold-smoking attachment. A, lid; B, food-rack; C, removable base of smoke-box (placed on wooden blocks for cold smoking); D, smoke compartment; E, stand for smoke compartment; F, cold-smoking attachment

around the raised base-plate, and around the baffle-plate if you use one, by which time, suitably cooled, it is in proper condition for cold smoking the food. (For the method of assembling the box, topping up the fuel and timing the smoking, see pages 105–11).

CHARCOAL SMOKE-COOKERS

This type of commercial smoke-cooker, whether on wheels or legs, is basically a heavy-gauge steel bowl with a concave lid. The finish, inside and out, is normally a rustproof porcelain enamel which will not burn or even stain. Dampers, which flick open or shut at a touch, control the air flow at the top and bottom of the appliance.

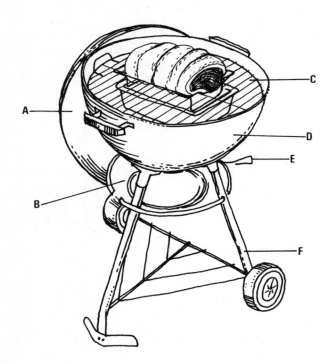

17 'Kettle' smoke-cooker (single, round bowl). A, concave lid with damper and wooden handle; B, ash catcher; C, smoking grid or food-carrier; D, bowl with wooden handles; E, handle of bottom damper and ash remover; F, aluminium legs with wheels

62

The 'kettle' model shown in drawing 17, which is made by Weber-Stephens Products Ltd, has the added refinement that the bottom vent-control on the damper also sweeps ash out of the smoker bowl into the ash-carrier beneath.

In this model, which can also be used for barbecuing, or for that matter stir-frying with the aid of a wok, the fire is made on the bottom grill of the bowl; then, when smoking is the order of the day, damp wood-chips and chunks are added to make the smoke. The food is then placed on a second nickel-plated grid or food-carrier which is laid on top of the smoking fire at bowl-rim level. Sometimes a pan of water is added to keep a joint such as a big turkey moist during its hours of cooking. The lid is then closed, and the food is smoke-roasted.

In another model with a three-part fire-bowl (made by Living Flair Ltd), the fire is made in one of the three bowls – it is left without a rim-rack so that the fuel can be topped up easily. No drip-tray is needed and flare-ups cannot occur since the fire is separated from the roasting foods (drawing 18).

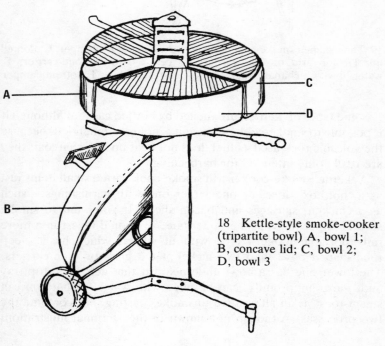

A
C
D
B

18 Kettle-style smoke-cooker (tripartite bowl) A, bowl 1; B, concave lid; C, bowl 2; D, bowl 3

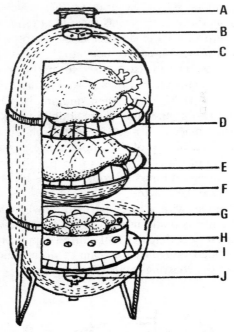

19 Tube-shaped smoke-cooker on legs. A, handle; B, damper; C, domed lid; D, top grid or food-carrier; E, centre grid or food-carrier; F, water-bowl; G, charcoal fuel; H, base grid; I, firebox; J, bottom damper

Some types of 'kettles' are fuelled by bottled gas, but although it is possible to smoke-cook on them it is not recommended, because the volcanic rock used as fuel does not heat up like charcoal; they are really only intended for barbecuing.

A 'kettle' smoke-cooker will smoke-cook varied small items just as a 'hot-box' does, or one larger one with garnishings – such as a chicken, sausages and bacon slices. If you want to smoke several larger items at the same time, you could invest in a more fully portable modern type without wheels which has a deep tube-shaped bowl, and two nickel-plated grids or food-carriers. The lower one has a bowl underneath it that acts as a drip-tray and, more importantly, can be filled with water so that you can steam-roast as an alternative to smoke-roasting – or combine the two processes. Although not shown in the sectional illustration, the smoke-cooker has a fire-door about two-thirds of the way down the side, for easy access to water and the charcoal heat source. The charcoal is put in a fire-box standing on a base grid. Flick-touch dampers top and bottom complete the smoke-cooker.

If you take off the lid and the water-bowl, and place the fire-box on the centre grid or food-carrier, you can also barbecue in this type of smoke-cooker. Smoke-cooking of this kind is like 'hot-box' smoke-cooking, but has the extra advantage of letting you cook larger pieces of food, in more varied ways. But the basic equipment costs much more (and so, of course, do big joints of meat and large poultry).

If you are beguiled by the thought of this sort of smoke-cooking, then decide whether the extra capacity of a smoke-cooker on legs, its easy refuelling and its big water-bowl for steaming food outweigh the advantages of a wheeled 'kettle', especially one with a flick-out ash-disposal mechanism and the facility for stir-frying that can be fun at picnics. Your choice really depends on where you want to cook, and on what occasions. A 'kettle' is ideal for a party, on a patio, by a swimming pool, or in the garden, for cooking one carvable joint or a lot of small steaks, chops or fish fillets. You could smoke-cook a turkey ahead of time, and carve it while guests barbecue other food. On the other hand, a smoke-cooker on legs – the model illustrated is Weber-Stephens' 'Smokey Mountain Cooker' – is probably more useful for weekend-cottage use, or for camping, or even as a second cooker at home if your ordinary kitchen stove is sometimes inadequate. Remember that neither provides any means of cold smoking.

A makeshift portable smoker

You can of course transport the materials for making a simple small smoker, set them up on your proposed site, and take them home again afterwards. For instance, a pierced iron bucket, charcoal and smoking fuel, four bricks, and a large sheet of heavy diamond aluminium foil can be assembled in moments as a makeshift hot smoker. Fill the bucket two-thirds full with charcoal, stand it on the bricks, with broken firelighter blocks scattered between them, and get the charcoal smouldering well. Then scatter the fuel to make smoke on the top. Find small thin straight green sticks on which to spit sausages you have brought along, small pieces of cooked meat or chicken breasts, or spit small fish you catch for yourself. Balance your makeshift spits on the rim of the bucket. Make a large cone or balloon-shaped cover of stiff diamond foil pierced with small holes and put it over the top of the bucket, overlapping the sides. It should be high enough to give plenty of headroom between the food and the cover.

This type of makeshift smoke-cooker cannot of course be relied on to give you properly cooked smoked food from the raw state; it will only impart a nice smoky flavour to already cooked food or to food that you can safely eat when only partly cooked.

IMPROMPTU SMOKER (SMOKE-COOKER) FOR PICNICS

You can use countryside materials to build a small temporary smoke-cooker – rocks, stones, branches, sand, turfs or a hollowed hillock – if you are somewhere where you will not be despoiling the countryside. How effective the smoke-cooker is depends on what you can find to use, and on what you wish to smoke and how. Most likely you will be wanting to smoke-cook food for a picnic or in camp, say fish you have caught or game which has fallen to your gun.

Any food tastes good to hungry hopefuls in the wilds, so even if it is slightly raw or charred the joy of outdoor eating will probably make up for it. A newly-caught fish will not have had time to decay and so will be harmless. However, if you would prefer to have properly cooked food without hassle, take along a portable smoke-cooker of some kind. The extra weight to carry will be compensated for by saving the time you would have had to spend on assembling do-it-yourself materials and building a makeshift smoker.

Many temporary smoke-cookers simply consist of a cave or framework of boughs, inside which the food is hung on sticks, with a fire lit underneath.

But endless variations are possible. The main hazards, however, are always the same: (a) that the smoke-cooker will leak badly; (b) that it may cause a fire; (c) that a furious farmer, keen shot or conservationist will berate you for spoiling the land/scent/countryside.

You can often stop leaks between stones or meshed branches by plastering them with mud or covering them with turfs. A canvas sheet is often recommended but is not a good idea, even if you are

in the habit of carrying one around: it may char or even catch fire –
branches can be drier than you think. Small fires can be doused,
like leaks, if you are vigilant.

But do remember that the least
carelessness can result in appalling spoilage if surrounding bushes
'catch'; a fire can get out of control in moments, with devastating
results to the countryside, to wildlife and to property. Do not be
surprised if an irate farmer, warden or local property-owner turns
you off the land; he has every right to be apprehensive.

10
A Preparation Room
for Serious Smoking

Although smoke makes smuts and soot, it's a mistake to think that, because of it, a scrap of dirt here or there makes no odds when food-smoking. Cleanliness is as vital as in any other branch of preparing food for table – or more so, since a good many smoked foods are eaten raw after processing.

Floors and walls where you process the food should be free from cracks and easy to wash. Even more important, only choose equipment which can easily be scalded or sterilised in some way. Make sure that china or earthenware vessels are not cracked and that enamelled ones are not chipped. The moving parts of a food processor or mincer are typical places where food scraps lurk, holding bacteria which may not be destroyed by smoking. Make sure they are kept scrupulously clean.

THE FOOD-PREPARATION SCENE

Types of meat, fish and other foods suitable for smoking are listed on page 115. This section describes the equipment you need for handling them.

Ideally, have a room separate from your domestic kitchen, if you are embarking on frequent or large-scale food preparation for smoking. Tile or put gloss paint on the walls, and fly-proof windows and doors. An easily washed floor is essential. For small-scale, intermittent smoking and 'hot-box' smoke-cooking, ordinary sturdy kitchen tools can be used, but for serious smoking keep a special set of tools in a place of their own.

You need two easily cleaned cutting boards, on which to cut up meat and process fish. A table in the centre of the room is usually more convenient for this kind of work than a work-top against a wall. Reserve a corner of it for foods such as eggs and cheese.

You need a thin-bladed boning knife, two or three short chef's kitchen knives, and if you will handle large meat joints yourself, a cleaver and a tenon saw. A long, narrow-bladed slicing knife and a pair of stout kitchen scissors will certainly be needed. For fish, you will also need one or two narrow-bladed filleting knives (one long, one short). To sharpen your knives, a knife sharpener or old-fashioned hone is required; knives must be kept razor-sharp and bright.

Don't forget a plastic dustbin and bags for trimmings, unwanted bones, fish-heads and egg-shells. Wiping and drying cloths and rolls of soft kitchen paper should be kept in a separate cupboard from ordinary kitchen stores.

Wooden skewers or thin pointed sticks will be needed to thread through split kidneys, small split fish and similar foods to keep them flat, or can be used for smoke-cooking kebabs. You will need stout smooth twine or cord and a large carpet or sailmaker's needle for threading through larger food items to make hanging loops.

After brining and drying (Chapter 11), many foods are better lightly oiled before smoking. Get a soft 1in/2.5cm brush and a smaller pastry brush, as well as a small bowl or jug to hold the oil. Some foods are better dry-spiced (page 127) before being smoked, and a spice rack or shelves to hold the spicing ingredients (and also the brining spices) should be allowed for in your smoke-kitchen plans and costs; a list of suggested spices to use is given on page 89. If you need to weigh or measure the spices (or the food), use the same scales as for preparing brine (page 71).

Sausage-making equipment (should you want to make your own smoked sausages) is described on page 139, as an optional extra.

BRINING EQUIPMENT

You have to dry salt, brine or pickle any food intended for cold and hot smoking before you smoke it, and probably some foods which will be smoke-cooked too, so brining (a useful, if incorrect, blanket term for them all) is given a whole chapter to itself (pages 77–93). Since you need equipment for these processes as soon as you start serious smoking, you should allow for the cost of it in your initial outlay; the basic items are described here.

Brining and pickling are easier to use for assorted shapes of meat joints and pieces than dry salting (page 81); so you will probably be sensible to invest in a brining or wet-cure bath for meat, and another for fish, first, and get a dry-salting 'bed' or tray later, if you must choose between them. Your bath for meats, which can be any trough-shaped container, should be large and deep enough to let you cover all the pieces of meat you are likely to want to brine at a time, both large and small. It must be made of heavy plastic, glass or earthenware, not of wood or bare metal, and it should if possible have a vent-hole with a spigot or tap low down on one side, or a drainage hole and plug in the bottom at one end, so that you can drain off the brine when required. An old-fashioned glazed earthenware sink is ideal. A similar shallower bath is suitable for fish.

For a dry-salting bed, buy a deep plastic tray, such as one intended for greenhouse use; make a hole in the bottom and fit it with a plug and an alternative cover of fine wire mesh for slow draining. The floor of your meat bath should slope so that large pieces of meat can be immersed at the lower end at the same time as small thin ones are soaked at the 'shallow end'. This is convenient because the thin pieces, which need less curing and must be taken out first, are easier to find and take out of shallow liquid. Tilt a flat-bottomed bath by putting one or two blocks under the end opposite the plug-hole.

Ideally, a bath with a draining hole at the bottom should stand on a sturdy frame or on a table with a hole cut in it so that the bath can be drained from underneath. If this is not possible, bale it out. Put the bath on a slate shelf or a concrete or tiled floor which is easily washed down. Messy drips are inevitable when removing food from the brine to the drying racks.

Acquire a large wooden board or tray which just fits inside the bath and which can be boiled, and two or three weights (eg large stones); these will hold down the food during brining. You will also need a large flameproof, non-metallic (eg enamelled) pan for boiling cooked brines, and a second one into which you can strain used brine. A large strainer will be needed for this. Get a pair of food tongs and a large broad spatula or peel for removing foods from the brine, and a long-handled spoon for stirring the brine.

Put the bath in a north-facing room or larder where you can keep the temperature around 38°F/3.5°C or lower. Keep a thermometer in the room, to check the temperature. A cellar, although often cool enough, is generally too damp and is seldom really airy. The room should get plenty of fresh air, although you must put screens on the windows to keep out flies, and take precautions to keep out pets and pests. You will also need blinds to keep the room fairly dark; the fat on meat is then less likely to turn rancid.

Newly-made brine or used brine can be stored in the same place as the brine bath, although if the weather is at all warm, it is better stored in a refrigerator in plastic containers with screw-on tops. If you have space, and can lay your hands on, a secondhand chilled cabinet from a delicatessen, it will be invaluable for storing not only brine but food awaiting brining and food ready for eating.

If possible, keep spices and other seasonings for brines and for dry-spicing together; many are the same. For measuring them, get a set of standard measuring spoons. You also need a good kitchen scale which records accurately in ounces/grams and in pounds/kilos on which you weigh both the brining ingredients and the foods before and after brining; and a large measuring jug or marked bucket for measuring water.

A fancier piece of equipment is a salinometer, which measures how dense your brine strength is; it is confidence-building although not strictly necessary (page 85).

Lastly you need a rail and hooks on which to hang the food while it dries off after brining, and a shallow tray to catch any drips from it. A free-standing commercial dress-rail is a good type to use, especially if it has castors and can be wheeled right up to the brine bath and then to the drying area. Otherwise, equip your drying area with hanging rails. In the drying place, allow plenty of rail space all on one level; or, if they are at two different heights, avoid placing one rail above another. Drips from food on an upper rail will make streaky stains on the surface of any food directly beneath it.

Equipping a suitable place for drying food after smoking is dealt with on page 74.

EQUIPMENT FOR SMOKING

You will need gear for supporting food in the smoker with minimal mess, and for handling the smoker during use and clearing up afterwards.

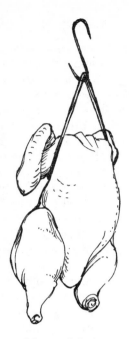

20, 21   Meat joint and bird strung for smoking and drying

Properly dried food (page 88) should make no mess when being cold smoked. If its fat begins to run, the fire is too hot. Your only problem is likely to be that any food hung directly on a hook or laid on a food carrier may stick to it (which is why traditionally cold-smoked joints and birds are strung up, as above).

The simple answer to this is to rub hooks, steel-mesh carriers, foil pans, rods, skewers and strings with a good-quality light oil, whether you are doing proper smoking or smoke-cooking. Use a piece of clean rag for applying it. Cover any baffle-plate directly below the food with heavy diamond aluminium foil, perforated if the baffle-plate itself has holes in it.

Do not lay soft items such as chicken livers directly on steel-mesh racks; they will bulge through the holes and stick messily to the half-buried wires. Oil them well and put them in perforated foil containers; oblong ones waste the least space.

As for firmer food items, see that they hang well clear of each other and of the drip-tray or baffle-plate below them. Keep them separate if laid on mesh carriers or racks – items which jostle each other will be patchily smoked.

A commercially built electric smoker is equipped with a temperature-gauge with a dial on the smoker door; if you are lucky enough to have one, it will help you to achieve perfectly smoked foods. If a smoker has a see-through door, as in some gas and electric cookers, an oven thermometer strategically placed inside serves the same purpose. Otherwise you must rely on 'before-and-after' weighing (page 78) to find out when your food is ready; when smoke-cooking in a kettle, a meat thermometer can be used.

When naturally moist foods are being smoke-cooked, they may exude moisture which collects on the inside of the smoker roof, adding to any acid condensation from the fuel. Acid condensation can be a real nuisance sometimes, because a film of blackish moisture collects on the smoker 'ceiling'. If the smoker has a lid which must be taken off to get at the food, as in a 'hot-box', drips of this moisture may be shaken off onto the food, and stain it. To lessen the risk, clean the inside of the lid thoroughly before use to remove any residual build-up of sooty smoke, and remove the lid very gently, with a piece of soft kitchen paper at hand to mop off any drips.

Cleaning up the smoker after use

Any old smoke-house is blackened inside with the dried smoke of years, and a new one should at least be 'seasoned' with smoke deposits (page 47) before you use it. These deposits are not 'dirty' and their faint pungency is certainly preferable to the smell of raw brick or concrete dust which might otherwise be carried in new smoke swirling round your food. Except for the moist acid deposits which may accumulate inside the lid of a small home-made smoker or smoke-box, leave them alone. All you need to remove are used fuels and any traces of food or grease.

How you do it will depend on what kind of smoker you have, but you only need ordinary household cleaning materials such as clean rags, washing-up and drying cloths, detergent and impregnated wire pads.

You will need to scrape unused fuel, ash, charred sawdust and any trickles of fat out of the fire-box, tray or pit. A flat-bottomed hand shovel, stiff hand brush and dustpan and a small coarse-meshed garden sieve for filtering ash from unused solid fuel will do most of the job, although you may need a wire brush, scraper or wire wool for any residues which stick.

A plastic sheet or garden 'donkey' may be useful to hold cold ash sieved out, which can then be removed to a rubbish-tip or compost heap (or dug into garden soil, if the smoker is sited in the garden).

Steel hooks, removable mesh carriers and any loose baffle-plate or drip tray should be washed in hot water with a good household detergent and wiped dry with soft kitchen paper before re-use. Any rods should be wiped and re-oiled, and dirty foil should be thrown away in a large rubbish bag.

Commercially built smokers and smoke-boxes are always supplied with an instruction manual detailing how to care for the equipment. Use the cleaning materials in the way described, to avoid any blame for defects if the appliance carries a guarantee.

DRYING AND STORAGE SPACE

You need a cool, but not cold, dry place for drying off your food after smoking it. The temperature should be even, around 55° −60°F/13°−16°C. In fair weather, you can dry off your food outdoors, provided there is only a slight breeze and the food is well protected from dust and flies. Indoors, windows will need fly-proofing and the floor and walls should be pest-proof. The floor must be easy to wash down, since the food may drip a good deal at first. A fan to create a draught in warm weather is useful.

For small-scale or intermittent smoking, you will prepare the food in a domestic kitchen, but drying off cannot be done there because the atmosphere is often too hot and steamy. An airy corridor may solve the problem, provided it is wide enough to take the rails of hanging food (page 71); they will not occupy it long. Remember that the food items must not be crowded together on the rails, and that you will be drying whole batches of food from the smoker at one time, so allow plenty of rail-space.

Smoke-cooked foods *must* be treated like fresh-cooked foods: put them in a refrigerator or chilled cabinet as soon as they have cooled, and eat them as soon as possible. Well-brined and smoked solid pieces of meat, whole or split poultry and whole fish can usually be stored safely for a short time without being frozen or chilled. The storage place should not receive direct sunlight, and its temperature should not be more than 41°F/5°C. A cool larder with stone shelves is ideal. It should be as pest-proof as you can make it; an old-fashioned wire mesh or muslin meat-safe or cover is a good food-protector. Remember that it is unwise to use a fly-spray near food.

A fan draught is not needed although the air should not be stagnant.

The food items should hang from rails or be laid on roasting or cake racks so that air can circulate all round them. If you have no meat cover, cover them loosely with foil or put them in porous bags or wrappings (not plastic). Large labels are needed, detailing when each piece of food was smoked, and giving an 'Eat By – ' date. Write on the labels in clear black ink with a felt pen – do not trust to memory.

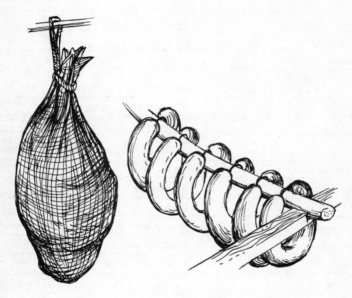

22 Meat joint and sausages hung for drying

KEEPING A RECORD

For successful smoking of any kind, adequate records are important. Obtain a large notebook in which to record the details of each smoking operation. Include the weights of food items before and after brining and smoking, any spices or other flavourings added to a brine or before smoking the food, the length of time you smoke it for, the smoking method and the type and approximate quantity of fuel used. Add the proposed storage method and time.

Food type/wgt	1 lb/450 g trout
Preparation	Whole
Wgt before brining (prepared)	14 oz/400 g
Wgt after brining	12½ oz/350 g
Brine recipe	Simple Fish Brine
Brining time	1 hour
Smoking method	Cold then hot smoking in Brooks smoker
Additions before smoking	None
Smoking time	10 hours (8 hrs cold)
Fuels	2 solid fuel tablets
	¼ charcoal pack, chips, 8 tablespoons smoking powder, handful hardwood chips
Wgt after smoking	11½ oz/310 g
Where stored	Refrigerator at 40 F/5°C
HQSL (estimated)	2 weeks
When eaten	After 1 week
How eaten	Cold, uncooked
Result	Colour and wgt OK, not tasty
Comment	Increase brining time 1 5 mins, smoking time 30 mins.

Sample page of record book

11
Brining and Brines

Salt cures (preserves) food all by itself. It does so by drawing liquid out of the food, and taking its place. Bacteria cannot operate in salt; the longer the food remains in contact with salt, the more saturated with salt it becomes, and so the longer and more safely that particular item will keep.

WHY FOOD IS CURED BEFORE SMOKING

We do not soak all our meat, fish and poultry in brine or rub them with salt before cooking them. There is no need, because the fairly high heat of baking, boiling or frying kills most of the harmful bacteria and makes the food safe to eat – for a short time. The same goes for smoke-cooked food, provided we eat it within a day of processing it.

Traditionally smoked foods are a different matter. Cold smoking means bathing food in smoke which is, by its nature, slightly warm for several hours at least. Bacteria like nothing better than slightly warm, moist food to breed in. Cold smoking unsalted food may encourage some which are smoke-resistant to breed in the moist centre of the food. Even the higher but moderate heat of hot smoking may not then kill them all off.

Besides this, brining and pickling create a wide variety of delicious flavours which smoke alone cannot provide, improve the food's texture, and give it a richly tinted, glossy surface.

HOW SALT WORKS

Salt is used for curing in three ways: as dry salt, as brine (salt and water), or mixed with water, sugar and spices to make a sweet cure or pickle. Since most wet 'cures' have other flavourings added to the salt, brining and pickling are often both called brining.

77

Sometimes, since dry salt becomes soggy by drawing liquid out of the food, all three methods are called 'brining' for convenience.

In traditional curing, salt enters the food from outside (it is not pumped in by injection), so it takes time to penetrate to the centre of the food. Thick pieces of a given food therefore take longer to cure than thin ones, given the same quantity of salt.

The rate at which liquid is exchanged for salt in food depends on how concentrated the salt is. When mixed with water in a brine, it dries out the food less quickly than undiluted salt; likewise a strong brine with a high salt content acts faster than a weak one or a pickle containing beer, treacle or spices as well as the salt.

It also depends on how cold the food is. It should be chilled to 38°F/3.5°C before curing and be kept at that temperature or very slightly lower, but it must not be frozen. Although salt acts more quickly at warmer temperatures, so do bacteria. On the other hand, curing too slowly may give bacteria a chance to develop in the centre of a thick piece of meat, and the cure won't work at all if the food is frozen.

As the salt replaces the liquid, the drying-out process hardens the food (rather like a dry sponge). Fat absorbs less salt than lean tissues, so fatty foods tend to stay softer as well as to taste less salty than lean products given the same treatment, although they may spoil more easily.

When food is fully saturated with salt, it is too hard and salty to eat, even after soaking. However, no food need be completely saturated with salt to protect it against spoilage; even quite a low salt content makes it safe to eat, at least for a short time. The problem is that you cannot tell, just by looking at it, how much salt a foodstuff has absorbed. How can you know when a particular food has absorbed enough salt to make it safe to eat, without spoiling its juiciness and flavour?

WEIGHT LOSS

Food loses weight (although not nutritional value) when its liquid is leached out by salt. The greater its weight loss, therefore, the longer it can be stored without refrigeration. However, in home curing and smoking, preserving for long storage without freezing or chilling would mean creating hard, salty products which would have to be soaked before being cooked and eaten. Even if you accept that, it is not wise to attempt it without experience or professional teaching.

Since there is, in any case, no need for most of us to undertake it today, experts have worked out what percentage of weight most types of fish and meat should lose to make them safe to eat at once (or frozen and thawed), yet still taste their best as salted, smoked products. By weighing a particular food before you salt and smoke it, you can therefore estimate fairly easily what its weight should be at the end to give you a product both safe and succulent.

The following weight losses will make any salted and smoked food safe to eat when it leaves the smoker, but it must then be frozen, refrigerated or else kept cold and eaten within a few days, unless a particular recipe says otherwise.

Most prepared fish lose between 13 and 20 per cent of their weight although some specially smoked products such as smoked cod's roe should lose 20–25 per cent. Chickens, turkeys, guineafowl and game birds should lose about 20 per cent; ducks, geese, butcher's meats and venison nearer 25 per cent.

But knowing this is not quite enough if you are going to both salt and smoke the food. You may like a lightly salted and very smoky flavour, or the other way round; so even before you salt it, you have to decide what flavour and weight loss you want the food to have when you *begin* smoking it. That will depend, not only on the type of food, its fat content and thickness, but on the type of salt you use for curing and the way you apply it.

TYPES OF SALT

Salt is made by evaporating sea-water or water mixed with rock salt from underground. The salt may consist of large or small crystals and contain about 1.5 per cent of other substances, depending on where it comes from and how it has been processed. Table salt is a fine, pure smooth-running type of salt but it is wastefully expensive to use for curing. Cheaper types are just as good or better.

The types most often used are:

Bay salt: a coarse hard salt with large crystals. It dries out food less than other types of salt because its big crystals mop up less surface moisture on the food.

Bar salt: this type is heated, pressed into moulds while still hot, then dried. The bars are sometimes crushed to make 'dairy salt' with finer crystals.

Common or kitchen salt: usually rock salt refined like table salt but without magnesium carbonate added to make it run freely. The crystals are fairly fine and easy to handle.

Vacuum salt: made from purified brine evaporated in closed containers without air. It has fine, small, even crystals, and is purer than the other types. This may make it seem the best to use, but it is heavier to handle, and its fine crystals tend to cake on the food's surface when it is used for dry salting. As the food dries out and shrinks, a space may be left between the caked salt and the food's surface, so the salt cannot do its work. For this reason, many craftsmen prefer to use a mixture of vacuum salt and one of the coarser types.

OTHER CURING INGREDIENTS

Besides salt, the curing ingredient mentioned most often in older recipes is saltpetre, or the quick-acting form of it called sal-prunella. Saltpetre turns meat rosy-pink when cooked instead of the dull grey colour given by salt alone. Some authorities now think saltpetre is dangerous to health, and as in any case it tends to harden flesh food, it is best omitted. The food's grey tint does no harm.

Other common curing ingredients are vinegar, alcohol in the form of wine, spirits or beer, treacle or honey used instead of sugar or with it, and pepper. Some of these, such as treacle, colour the food as well as flavouring it and helping to preserve or soften it.

Most other curing ingredients such as spices are only added for flavouring, as in a marinade. (In fact some marinades are very like wet-curing mixtures.)

TYPES OF CURE

In the old days your curing method would have been influenced by where you lived. In some parts of Britain, for instance, people used dry-salting because the local fat pork needed a strong cure; others used a wet cure because pickling ingredients such as beer or cider were made locally and were easy and cheap to buy. Since it was pickled and kept in large barrels, wet-cured pork was known as 'barrel' pork.

Salt, alone or with other ingredients, is used to cure food in several ways.

Dry cures

1 Sprinkle the food with a little salt fairly often. The food gives out only a little liquid at a time and loses weight only slowly, but the process is easy to control. It is suitable for delicate, small, moist pieces of food, such as fresh cod's roe, that might disintegrate in brine (full directions on page 123).

2 Sprinkle the food with plenty of salt; it will draw out a lot of liquid. Unless you remove this you will end up with almost the same kind of wet cure as when using brine. However, if your salting tray has a drain and you let the brine drain away, the effect will be similar to that of dry packing (see below). For meat, this can be varied by using a rubbing technique (page 83).

3 Pack the food down into a bed of dry salt and cover it with more salt. All the liquid drawn out is absorbed by the salt, so the food does not reabsorb any. This curing method is called dry packing.

Wet cures

1 Soak the food in a strong solution of salt and water (brining).

2 Soak the food in a (usually) weaker solution with spices and other flavourings added, often including sugar (pickling).

There is one other choice. In traditional curing, larger pieces of meat are often rubbed well with dry salt two or three times a day for several days and then pickled. The dry salt rub starts the curing, so that the meat contains less liquid to dilute the brine. This method also protects the meat quickly against bacteria.

DRY CURING

Dry curing draws more liquid out of food in a given curing time, so it shortens the time the food must stay in the smoker afterwards. It also saves at least some of the handling of heavy buckets of water or brine. It is excellent – and quick – for flat smooth pieces of food, especially fish. Dry packing in particular also protects raw meat foods better against bacteria in hot weather, especially when you have difficulty in keeping down the temperature of the brining place to 38°F/3.5°C.

If you prefer food such as white fish with only a mild smoked flavour, or want to speed up the smoking process, you may prefer to use a dry cure.

Dry salting has had some strong supporters: William Cobbett, the famous journalist, suggested in 1820 getting 'a salting trough which has a gutter round its edges to drain away the brine for to have sweet and fine bacon the flitches must not be sopping in brine, which gives it the sort of taste that barrel pork and sea junk have than which there is nothing more villainous. Therefore change salt often and let it melt and sink in but let it not lie too long.' He was of course writing about preserving pork for storage all winter long.

Dry curing method 1

Sprinkle a layer of fine salt all over the bottom of an earthenware, plastic or ceramic platter or shallow dish in which the pieces of food can lie without touching each other. (For a short-cut method, spread four layers of soft kitchen paper over the bottom instead of salt.) Lay the food on the salt (or paper). Sprinkle it with enough salt to cover it lightly. Leave it at a temperature of 38°F/3.5°C for 8 to 12 hours. Lift off the food, remove the damp salt or paper, and re-sprinkle or re-cover the bottom of the dish. Replace the food, with the salted surface underneath. Sprinkle with salt again. Repeat the whole process daily, turning the food over each time, until the salt or paper under the food is dry. Rinse the food briefly under a cold running tap and pat dry; hang it and dry it off for a few hours only. Then weigh the pieces, oil them, and cold smoke them lightly; they will shrivel if over-smoked or hot smoked.

Dry curing method 2

Use a deeper dish with a mesh-covered drain in which two or three layers of thin pieces of fatty fish or meat can be stacked; fish should be split or filleted. Rub or sprinkle them well with fine salt. Sprinkle the dish with about 1in/2.5cm of fine salt all over. Lay one or more pieces of food on the salt bed side by side. Sprinkle with a layer of salt ½in/1cm thick on the thicker parts of the food, but only a fine sprinkling on the thin tail end of a fish. Repeat the layers if you wish. Cover the top layer with a good ½in/1cm salt, then lay on top a sterilised board and a light weight. Leave at a temperature of 38°F/3.5°C until the food has lost a good deal of liquid. The time can vary from 1 hour for thin fish fillets to 18 hours for a large split salmon or 3 – 4 days for a thick slice of pork. Rinse the food to remove surface salt, and weigh. Then oil and smoke.

A variation of this method for thicker pieces of pork meat, especially, is to use mixed fine and coarse salt, allowing about 1lb/450g mixed salt for each 10lb/4.5kg pork pieces. Place the meat in a deep earthenware, plastic or ceramic dish and rub well with half the salt. Keep at 38°F/3.5°C for 3 days. Repeat the rubbing, using the remaining salt, then leave to cure. Turn the meat over two or three times while curing. Drain, rinse and dry off, then weigh and smoke. See page 87 for curing times.

There are other traditional variations for meat, using a spiced dry-salting mixture, and rubbing the meat with one-third of the mixture each time.

Dry curing method 3 (dry packing – meat and poultry)

Use pieces of meat weighing not more than 6½lb/3kg each, and of the same thickness (at least 1in/2.5cm thick). Measure and note the thickness. Before curing, clean any pieces of meat with bone or corners by soaking in strong brine. Make the brine by mixing 2¼ UK gallons/10 litres boiling water with 6½lb/3kg salt (2¼ US gallons with 5¼lb salt). When the salt has dissolved, put the meat in it for 15 – 30 minutes, depending on thickness. Remove and drain on soft paper. (The brine need not be wasted; it will make a wet cure by adding ¾ gallon/3½ litres (7½ US pt) water to it.)

For the dry-salting mixture, use one-tenth of the weight of the meat in coarse and fine salt, mixed. Divide the salt mixture into three equal portions: one for rubbing, one for sprinkling, and one for repacking. Rub the meat pieces with one portion, more lightly on the flesh side than skin side, and more heavily round any bone ends and into the bone hollow. Rub birds inside and out, under the wings and inside the thighs.

Prepare a 2in/5cm thick bed of plain dairy or similar salt, if possible, in a container which will hold the meat pieces in 1 or 2 layers without touching. Press the pieces of meat into it, skin-side down. Sprinkle them with the second portion of mixed salt. Then cover with 2in/5cm plain dairy salt, packing it tightly close to the meat at the sides. Leave at 38°F/3.5°C for 2 – 3 days for thin pieces, 4 – 6 days for thick ones.

Break up the salt covering and remove any damp and discoloured salt. Sprinkle the meat with the last portion of mixed salt, and repack with plain salt; if layered, put the pieces you want first on top. Leave for up to 4 days per 1in/2.5cm thickness of meat in all. If left longer, the meat will be fully cured with quite a hard salty cure, and will need soaking before use (which will destroy some of its smoky flavour). Do not leave any meat, however thick or fatty, in a cure for longer than 4 weeks, less in hot weather.

You can take pieces of meat out of the salt bed at any time after a week in salt. Each time you remove a piece, repack the rest tightly if disturbed, so that all the meat is in contact with salt.

Rinse the meat you take out to remove surface salt, and dry off. Cold smoke, and then hot smoke if you wish.

WET CURING: BRINE AND PICKLES

Wet curing diffuses dissolved salt (brine) gently through the food, blending it with the food's own fluid, so the food is made less hard and salty-tasting than in dry curing. It is also a more flexible method as large and small pieces of meat can be cured at the same time, or some pieces cured for a short time and others for longer in the same brine. It can be used for most types of fish and meat, in pieces of all shapes and sizes.

Dry salting is not ideal, for instance, for meat joints on the bone, or foods with wrinkled skins and cavities. The salt may not reach into every crevice, and bacteria can then continue to lurk there; such foods must be given a brief soak in a strong cleansing brine before being dry salted. Dry salting is also a wasteful method of curing thick knobbly meat joints or birds, which need a deep layer of salt to cover them. (They are best rubbed with salt, then wet cured.) Also, wet curing gives you a wider choice of flavours, since you can use vinegar, treacle, honey, wine or beer to make a pickle. Sugar tenderises flesh, so a sweet wet cure is good for tougher meat, elderly poultry or game birds. It also gives a flavour to bland foods that suits modern tastes.

The main disadvantage of traditional wet curing is that the salt may take a long time to reach the centre of a thick or close-grained piece of meat or a large bird, which is why professional and experienced craftsmen use a brine pump. This can be a useful piece of equipment if you are curing large pieces of meat, especially with a bone in. Inject the brine right into the centre of the meat around the bone, which is where harmful bacteria are most likely to breed. The injection of salt deals with them quickly. The disadvantage of using the pump is that unless it is scrupulously clean extra bacteria can be introduced into the meat with the needle. Therefore sterilise it both before and after use.

The pump is filled and used exactly like a hypodermic syringe, using about 2 tablespoons brine per 1lb/450g meat.

The brine pump does not save you any curing time. The meat must still be cured in the ordinary way, and you should aim for the same weight loss. But it does make you feel safer when curing ham, venison and other big joints 'on the bone'.

Making a basic brine

First boil the water for the brine or pickle if it is heavily chlorinated or if you doubt its absolute cleanliness. Cool it well before use.

When you start making the brine, bring about one-third of the water to the boil, add the salt, turn off the heat and stir until dissolved. Add this brine to the remaining water. Cool, put into the brine bath and stir well.

Water containing 3lb 7oz (1.7kg) salt per UK gallon (4.5 litres), or 2lb 14oz per US gallon, at room temperature is called a 100 per cent saturated brine; it can hold no more dissolved salt. This is too much salt for modern tastes. You can make your basic brine any strength you like, but most craftsmen recommend a 70–80 per cent plain brine solution, made with 2lb 10oz (1.1kg) per UK gallon (4.5 litres) (or 2lb 4oz per US gallon). Check the density of the brine by floating a salinometer in it if you have one, or a freshly peeled juicy potato – it should just float. This is especially important before you re-use a brine, because otherwise you will have to top up its salt content by guesswork.

Never use the same brine for fish and meat, either together or one after the other.

Brine or pickle can be re-used provided it does not contain blood and is sweet and clean; if it only contains a few 'bits', strain them out. Throw it away, however, if it smells sour or is at all scummy. Before re-using it, top up the salt and other ingredients in proportion.

Flavoured brines (pickles)

Salt is in fact seldom used just by itself. Other ingredients are usually added, particularly sugar, making what is called a pickle. When pickling, you generally use less salt than a 70 per cent solution. Use the recipes below as a guide to quantities.

Boiled pickles: many sweet-flavoured brines (pickles) are boiled or 'cooked' to dissolve the flavouring ingredients and to make them keep better. Sometimes all the ingredients are boiled together, skimmed well, and cooled to 38°F (3.5°C). Otherwise the flavourings (except for sugar) are boiled in about 1pt (550ml/1¼ US pt) of the water for 15 minutes and then cooled to 35°F (2°C). The liquid is strained off into the unflavoured water, and any solid ingredients are tied in clean muslin and added. Sugar is then stirred in.

A cooked pickle can be re-used, but must be reboiled with a little extra salt and sugar before re-use, or after 5 weeks if not used. It can be reboiled again with a little more sugar and salt before being used once more, or after another 5 weeks, if clean; but after that use, it must be thrown away. Never reboil a brine more than twice. After boiling make sure it is really cold (38°F (3.5°C)) before using it. If at any time it becomes sour, 'ropy' or shows any sign of white mould on the surface, throw it away.

Store brine or pickle in screw-top plastic containers, at not more than 38°F (3.5°C), in a refrigerator, chilled cabinet or cold room.

Brining method

Weigh the pieces of meat or fish to be cured. Estimate and record the brining times for the various weights (see below). Allow longer for thick and fatty pieces.

Pack the pieces of meat or fish into a prepared tilted brining bath (page 70), thin pieces at the shallow end, thick pieces such as meat joints at the deep end. Cover completely with prepared, cold brine or pickle at not more than 38°F (3.5°C). Put a sterilised board or wooden tray on top and weight it down to keep the food under the surface of the cure. Leave for the estimated time, then remove, dry off and weigh. (If you need meat in a hurry, you can take a piece out partly pickled and smoke-cook it.)

Check the condition of the brine every day. If food is in cure for more than two days, *overhaul* the brine every third day. Overhauling means giving the brine a good stir up, to make sure all parts of the food are soaked, and to prevent the heavier flavouring ingredients sinking to the bottom, leaving a weak pickle above.

If necessary, remove some pieces of food temporarily to let you overhaul the brine thoroughly. Take meat pieces out with tongs, not a fork, to avoid any blood seeping into your brine when they go back. Take out small goods with a spatula or peel.

Brining times

The time your food stays in brine is, within limits, a matter of your own choice. Some people like a much saltier flavour than others. Again, some prefer to get their chosen flavour by using a strong brine for a short time, while others prefer to use a weaker brine or pickle and to soak the food for longer.

The time varies too, of course, with the type of food, its fattiness and how much cut surface is exposed to the brine. Fish fillets take a very short time compared with whole fish in their skins.

As a rule, it is better for a beginner to under-brine than over-brine. You can make up the desired weight loss during smoking if necessary, whereas an over-salty flavour spoils the product.

Meat, being compact, accepts a much wider range of brining times and brine strengths than fish with its more delicate texture and flavour; and it always needs much longer brining than either fish or birds. As a very general guide, start by giving moderately fatty butcher's meats, which have been well hung and chilled, 2 days for each lb/450g of their weight in a standard brine or pickle.

Treat an ox tongue (beef tongue) or heart in the same way.

A really thick compact meat joint, such as a leg of pork or a piece of elderly, tough beef or venison, should have longer in cure, say 3 days per lb/450g, and so should very fatty meat. Shorten the time for very lean pieces of meat, especially thin tender ones such as beef fillet.

Meat purchased for home-made sausages is often brined before making them. Some complete sausages are brined before smoking, or are dry salted, but only briefly because the undiluted salt dries out the sausage-meat mixture rapidly.

Poultry and game birds need not take long to brine. Most kinds up to 4lb/2kg in weight smoke well after 2 – 3 hours per lb/450g in a standard brine, although a large duck needs at least 3½ hours. Dry-fleshed birds such as guineafowl will take less time than average, and tiny birds such as quail can be brined in an hour.

Some skilled craft food-smokers brine for only a third of these times, while others brine in a sweet weak pickle for three times as long. This shows how wide your choice of brining times can be, given different cures, smoking methods and tastes.

It is tricky to estimate brining times for fish, since these differ according to whether the fish are white or oily, large or small, and whether they are skinned, split or filleted. Some, such as kippers and buckling, are processed in a special way, as are salmon and all small shellfish. It is best to refer to good standard individual brining and smoking recipes, rather than try to follow any general guide.

Drying off

Drying off most foods is important because it gets rid of excess moisture from the brining, so shortening the smoking time. Also, while drying, the food gains a glossy surface texture called the pellicle, which helps to give it its golden colour when smoked and may help the smoking process.

Drain the food well, and rinse it to remove excess surface salt, then pat it dry. Hang it or lay it on racks in a dry airy place (page 71), but not in a strong draught which will harden the surface. It should be well protected from dust and pests. The pieces of food should not touch each other; let air circulate round them freely. Since they may drip, place a shallow tray under them if they are indoors.

The time they take to dry depends on their size and type, the way they have been brined and the weather. Small, naturally dry pieces of food may only take 3 – 4 hours, but most fish need 12 – 18 hours to dry, and poultry, game birds and meats take 24 hours at least.

If the food has been heavily salted, a white layer of salt may appear on its surface as it dries. Wipe if off as soon as it appears.

COMMON FLAVOURINGS FOR BRINES AND FOODS
FOR SMOKING

White or soft brown sugar, clear
  honey, golden syrup, black
  treacle
Ale or beer
Allspice berries
Bay leaves, fresh or dried
Cardamom seeds
Celery salt
Cider (dry)
Cinnamon sticks
Cloves, whole or crushed
Coriander seeds
Cumin seeds
Dill seeds
Garlic – whole, crushed or squeezed
  cloves, or as garlic salt or powder
Ginger root, fresh and sliced or in
  slivers, or ground
Juniper berries
Lemon and Pepper Seasoning
  (McCormick's)

Lemon rind or juice
Mace, whole blade or ground
Mixed spice, ground
Mustard, whole seeds or as dry
  mustard
Nutmeg, in fragments or ground
Onion, whole, or chopped, or as
  onion salt or powder
Paprika, hot or mild
Pepper, white or black (whole or
  ground)
Pickling spice, bought or home-
  made
Poultry Seasoning (McCormick's)
Rosemary, sprigs or leaves
Soy sauce
Tabasco
Turmeric
Vinegar, white (mild) or red
Wine, white or red
Worcestershire sauce

23 Flavourings for cures and smoke-cooking

RECIPES FOR BRINES AND PICKLES

There are hundreds of recipes for brines and pickles. Try some of them as well as this small, basic selection. Even more rewarding, make up your own.

To make larger quantities of pickle than given below, increase all the ingredients in proportion.

Simple fish brine/pickle

1 gallon	4.5 litres	fresh water	20 cups
1½oz	35g	onion salt	4tbsp
1½oz	35g	garlic salt	4tbsp
1lb	450g	salt	1¾ cups
4 – 6oz	100 – 175g	brown sugar	4 – 6oz
3 – 4fl oz	75 – 100ml	strained lemon juice	⅓ – ½ cup

Boil the water, and cool slightly. Dissolve the salts and sugar in the water. Cool completely and strain in lemon juice to taste, depending on type of fish. Use cold. Covers 8 medium-sized whole fish.

Note: Onion and garlic salt may need to be creamed with a little water before mixing since they do not dissolve easily.

Brine for salmon (or similar fish)

1 gallon	4.5 litres	fresh water, boiled and cooled to tepid	20 cups
3 – 4	3 – 4	bay leaves (optional)	3 – 4
8 – 10	8 – 10	juniper berries (optional)	8 – 10
2tbsp	30ml	onion salt	2tbsp
1lb	450g	salt	1¾ cups
1oz	25g	brown sugar or clear honey	3tbsp
3 – 4fl oz	75 – 100ml	strained lemon juice	⅓ – ½ cup

Boil 1pt/550ml (2½ cups) of the water, and soak the spices if used for 20 minutes. Meanwhile dissolve both salts in the remaining water. Stir in the sugar or honey and dissolve. Strain in the flavoured liquid, tie the spices in a scrap of muslin, and add to the brine. Chill before use.

Sweet brine for salmon or other fish

1 gallon	4.5 litres	fresh water	20 cups
8oz	225g	black treacle (molasses)	¾ cup
2tbsp	30ml	onion salt	2tbsp
2tbsp	30ml	garlic salt (optional)	2tbsp
1lb	450g	salt	1¾ cups
3 – 4fl oz	75 – 100ml	strained lemon juice (or to taste)	⅓ – ½ cup
2tbsp	30ml	dill seeds	2tbsp
		rum to taste	

Heat the treacle in its container to make measuring easier. Cream the onion and garlic salt if used with a little of the water. Mix all the ingredients well. Bring to the boil, stir, then leave to cool completely. Chill before use.

Brine for liver, kidneys, hearts, game steaks

Use the Sweet Brine for Salmon (above), but substitute 3fl oz/75ml (⅓ cup) red wine or sherry and water for the rum. Instead of dill seeds, use 6 juniper berries, 2 bay leaves and 3 allspice berries.

General-use sweet brine

For beef (large and small pieces), tongue, poultry (chicken, turkey, guineafowl) and game birds

2 – 4 gallons	9 – 18 litres	boiled, cooled water	2½ – 5 gallons
2oz	50g	pickling spice	2oz
2½lb	1.2kg	salt	2½lb
8oz	225g	brown or white sugar	1⅓ cups

Put the pickling spice into 1pt/550ml (2½ cups) of the water. Bring to the boil, remove from the heat and leave to stand for 15 minutes. Mix the salt into the remaining water, strain in the flavoured liquid and return the spice tied in a scrap of muslin. Stir until the salt dissolves, then stir in the sugar and dissolve by stirring. Chill before use.

Treacle and ale pickle for pork
Cures 4 × 2lb/900g pieces belly of pork (bacon pieces)

		coarse salt for rubbing	
1pt	550ml	light ale (beer)	2½ cups
1pt	550ml	stout (strong beer)	2½ cups
1½lb	675g	black treacle (black molasses)	1½lb
12oz	335g	fine salt	12oz
12oz	335g	coarse salt	12oz

Choose pieces of meat of the same thickness. Rub them all over with coarse salt. Put them in a brine bath, and leave for 24 hours. Meanwhile boil all the ingredients together gently for 5 minutes, and leave to get quite cold. Pour the pickle over the meat. Keep in a cool place (38°F/3.5°C) until the end of the curing time (not more than 3 weeks), turning the meat and rubbing it with the cure daily. Drain and dry off.

Treacle brine for duck, goose and game birds

1 gallon	4.5 litres	fresh water	20 cups
8oz	225g	black treacle (molasses)	½lb
2tbsp	30ml	onion salt	2tbsp
1	1	large clove garlic	1
1lb	450g	fine salt	1¾ cups
2fl oz	50ml	rice vinegar or other mild white vinegar	¼ cup
2	2	bay leaves	2
2	2	whole cloves	2
¼pt	150ml	red wine	½ cup + 2tbsp
		brandy to taste	

Heat the treacle in its container until liquid to make measuring easier. Cream the onion salt in a little of the water. Peel and split the garlic clove. Mix all the ingredients and bring to simmering point. Stir well, remove from the heat, cool and chill before use.

Note: You can also use this brine for oddments such as liver or kidneys, which you may have room to smoke in an empty corner when smoking more solid pieces. Brine them in small foil pans, separately from the main items, and discard the brine after use.

Pickle for furred game

1 gallon	4.5 litres	fresh water	20 cups
9½oz	260g	salt	1 cup
2½oz	65g	soft light brown sugar	2½oz
2tsp	10ml	juniper berries	2tsp
3	3	fresh bay leaves	3
½tsp	2.5ml	whole coriander	½tsp
4½tsp	22.5ml	wine vinegar	4½tsp

Boil the water, and cool slightly. Mix the salt and sugar and dissolve them in the water. Stir in the juniper, bay and coriander. Cool completely, then stir in the vinegar. Use cold. Overhaul (page 87) every third day if needed.

12
Cold Smoking

There is no such thing as cold smoke because at least some heat is needed to produce smoke at all: but the heat used in cold smoking is so gentle that although the food is soaked in smoke, eventually right to the centre, it is never cooked. (In cook's language, it is a cold process because it is more like marinating the food in smoke than giving it heat treatment, ie cooking.)

KEEPING THE SMOKE COOL

Today we aim to keep some of the food's natural juiciness: cold smoking is the only way to do this and to permeate the food with the smoke's flavour at the same time. Any kind of hot smoking (see next chapter), like any kind of cooking without liquid, stiffens the food's surface so that no more flavour can get inside and no more liquid can get out. For these reasons alone, it is vital to keep the cold-smoking heat low, between 50°F and 85°F (10.0°C and 29.5°C). Most craftsmen have their own preferred temperature within this range for cold smoking each type of food, but if in doubt, the cooler the smoke the better, and certainly it should not get hotter than 90°F (32°C). A temperature between 70°F and 80°F (21.5°C and 26.5°C) can be used for most foods, but you need not worry if it drops during smoking; the process will take longer, that's all.

On the other hand, if the temperature rises above around 85°F (29°C), there is some risk that the food's surface will case-harden (stiffen) or that fish will soften inside as in prolonged cooking and will disintegrate. A sad waste of your precious salmon or trout!

Never try to hurry cold smoking. Control the temperature as far as possible by keeping the fire low and by adjusting the dampers or baffles which control the smoke flow.

Watch the quantity of smoke. Too much smoke can damage

94

your food in several ways; not least, it may be too hot, simply because there is so much of it. You do not want to keep the volume of smoke down to a trickle because the food may dry out before it gets enough smoke flavour, and there is a risk that it may be patchily smoked. But you do need to keep it to a reasonable quantity which will keep moving and escape quickly through your top outlets, not a sullen mass which clings around the food. It is therefore always important to deal with an over-enthusiastic fire quickly. Remove any large logs (these should not be used on a cold-smoking fire anyway), or sprinkle the fire with cool ash. In an emergency, use some earth, sand or cinders; do not use water, especially if you want to raise the heat later to hot smoke the food. You do not want humid smoke; it will slow down the smoking process and may spoil the food.

Use the same techniques for an over-hot charcoal fire as a wood one, reducing the quantity of fuel and sprinkling with ash or cinders. Reduce the level of gas or electric heating.

Factors which you cannot control and which may affect the temperature or quality of your smoke are the temperature and the humidity of the outside air. Their effect will of course be more marked if you are using a portable smoker outdoors than if you have a large shed-like brick kiln or have built a smoker under cover. Take particular care to keep the smoke temperature low in hot weather; and do not worry if it seems too low on a frosty morning. It won't be.

Assessing the temperature
An electric kiln or smoker has a built-in temperature gauge with a dial on the door which tells you the temperature inside. In any home-built smoker, assessing the temperature is much more difficult unless you have built or assembled one with a see-through door, and can place an oven thermometer inside where you can peep at it; put it near the top of the smoker, if possible on the top rack. If you are quick-fingered, you may be able to put an oven thermometer on the top rack of a smoker without a see-through panel, and hook it out through a damper outlet or a hole made specially; read the temperature instantly before it falls.

Beyond that, experience is likely to be your most reliable guide. Once you have found a type and quantities of fuel which give you results you like, record the details and stick to them.

HOW LONG TO SMOKE?

Within limits, smoking times are largely a matter of your own choice, although you must, of course, be guided by the weight and density of the food when you put it into the smoker, as well as the temperature and volume of the smoke, in deciding how long it will take to reach the final weight you want it to be. The more smoke the food gets, the stronger its smoked flavour will be. If you like a strong, smoked flavour, you can leave most meat or poultry in the smoker for a bit longer than it strictly needs. Smoking times of fish, especially white fish, are more critical because they are easily over-smoked.

In calculating any smoking times, allow oily fish quite a bit longer in the smoker than white fish. Note that rich fatty duck or goose needs a good deal longer than lean chicken, guineafowl and game birds. The thick compact flesh of turkey takes even longer to smoke properly. Do not under-smoke any minced-meat mixture, such as sausage-meat or hamburgers.

All butcher's meats take a lot longer to smoke than any other kind of food, and they are generally more adaptable about the length of time they need. Extra smoking for an hour or two generally does them no harm, whereas it ruins fish. Remember, though, that thin pieces of meat take less time to smoke than smaller thick chunks of the same initial weight, and lean beef takes a lot less time than fatty pork. It is really quite difficult to over-smoke pork – luckily, because you must *not* under-smoke it.

It would be helpful when you first start smoking to have some definite guide to the number of smoking hours for different types of food; but so many variable factors come into play that, in each case, the minimum and maximum smoking times are far apart. You must take into account not only the size and weight of the food pieces, but their shape, fat-covering and solidity, how many pieces you smoke at a time and how crowded they are in the smoker. The time is affected even more by the temperature of the smoke and how it varies from time to time, by the kind of heat and fuel which supply it, the efficiency of the smoker, and whether the weather is warm or cold, dry or damp. Sides of salmon, for instance, may take anything from 18 – 60 hours to smoke (in a smoke-box the time may be as little as 8 hours).

Your best plan, to start with, is to watch any food carefully the first time you smoke it, judge whether it is ready from its colour and surface texture, and test-weigh a sample piece (allow for the fact that it has not yet been dried off). Even experienced craft food-smokers have to do this when they try a new foodstuff. You can return it to the smoker if it doesn't seem to be ready. If it does, give it a final test by splitting it or making a cut in the thickest part, right to its centre, to see if it is smoked right through.

You will soon find, as you become more experienced, that you take the variable factors into account automatically, and estimate the smoking times of your familiar products accurately almost by instinct. Then you can begin to consider yourself a real craftsman, and can have confidence in your skill as well as in the products you produce.

STEP-BY-STEP GUIDE TO COLD SMOKING

1 Choose the foods you will smoke in one batch. All the brined dried pieces of food to be smoked at the same time should, if possible, be of the same type, and similar in weight and size. However, if you want to smoke, say, sprats and a single row of mackerel at the same time, or chicken livers with split chickens, it can be done; hang up the larger items and lay the small ones, blanched if necessary on racks (page 123) below, naked or in foil containers. Any drips from the same type of food will not matter on items such as sprats (but don't smoke cheese under fish or meat unless you like spotted cheese).

2 You will already have prepared the food for hanging in the smoker (pages 119–132) in order to hang it up to dry off after salting. The next step, therefore, is to weigh the pieces of food. Record any weights over 2oz/50g. Smaller items such as shellfish or chicken livers can't be assessed for readiness by weight so you have to follow individual recipes or your own judgment.

3 Prepare the smoker. Cover a drip-tray or baffle-plate at the bottom with foil if necessary, and see that your starting fuels are to hand and reasonably dry. Lay a fire if that will be your main heat source. Oil rods, hooks, racks and foil trays if you use them. Check that dampers or baffles move smoothly and easily. Make any other preparations your particular type of smoker requires; for instance remove a top rack if hanging long items.

4 Light your fire or start up whatever heat source you use. In

many smokers you need to get a wood or charcoal fire going well before adding the smoking fuel, and even in others it takes time for the heat to produce enough smoke to fill the smoker.

5 Load the smoker with the food items. Make sure that smoke can circulate round each piece. It is better to keep some food items chilled and smoke them later than to risk overcrowding the smoker. Pieces smoked too close together will have a poor colour and flavour.

If the smoke is not yet flowing freely, the brined dried food will come to no harm. Time the smoking period from when the smoke is swirling around it well.

6 Decide when you should first inspect the fuel to see if it needs topping-up. If you set yourself a timetable, you can check the state of the fuel at regular intervals – it is all too easy to forget it!

When solid foods are being smoked for a day or more, it does not matter, in fact, if the fire goes out provided you can estimate fairly accurately when the smoke-flow ceased so that you can recalculate the total smoking time. In fact some craftsmen take solid joints out of the smoker deliberately sometimes, to 'sweat' them for 12 – 24 hours to speed their weight loss.

However, you should, barring accidents, smoke small products gently but continuously until they are ready to come out of the smoker. Therefore, if smoking will go on overnight, arrange to top up the fuels just before you go to bed with enough materials to keep them smouldering overnight. This is when a charcoal fire has an advantage over wood, because you can pile extra lumps or briquettes on top. Sawdust is in fact the ideal smoking fuel for overnight smoking; if you remove charred dust, the 'live' smouldering dust will ignite quite a large pile of fresh dust placed on top of it.

7 Inspect the food from time to time while smoking, to turn it over if needed, and to make sure that no untoward disaster has occurred such as a fish coming adrift from its hook. It is also important to make sure that everything is going the way you want it. If the food looks fully coloured some time before the end of the smoking period, remove some of the smoking fuel and leave it to continue drying in the smoker to achieve its required weight loss with little or no actual smoke. Give it a bit longer than you would otherwise. On the other hand, if the food items are not picking up enough colour, you may want to add some hardwood shavings or

some other quick smoke-producing fuel, and give the food a greater volume of smoke for a short while. You want to end up with deep golden fish, russety-pink salmon sides or cod's roe, deep amber or chestnut meat.

As a rule, add any fragrant burning herbs or woods shortly before the end of the smoking time.

8 If the food is hanging up, items at the sides of most home-built smokers will usually be ready before those in the middle. If the food is on racks, items on the top rack will be done before those on the lower ones, and must be removed first. Just *before* the end of your estimated smoking time for the first batch, remove a sample product for closer inspection and test-weighing, especially if you are not 100 per cent sure how your fire has behaved or what volume and temperature of smoke the food has been subjected to throughout smoking: it may be ready sooner than you think.

Replace the item in the smoker if not yet ready. You may have to lose one small fish if you split it to see if it is smoked through (page 97), but this is better than losing a whole batch through under- or over-smoking. You needn't waste it; it will probably make a small quantity of excellent pâté.

9 Remove all the food from the smoker when it is ready. Weigh it to check its weight loss. Smother the fire (or riddle unburned fuel, eg charcoal, for re-use). Remove all the fuel.

10 All food items develop flavour by being dried off again after smoking, if only for a few hours (in the case of white fish). Some foods, eg salmon, *must* be matured for at least 24 hours, and most meats should be kept at least as long before eating. A ham may need 3 – 4 days' maturing. Hang or lay the items in the drying space, exactly as when drying off after brining.

STORAGE

If it has achieved its full weight loss (page 79), cold-smoked fish should keep for at least 36 hours, if well covered; most other foods should keep for at least 48 hours after they have matured before they need be eaten or else chilled or frozen – provided they are kept in a cool (50°F/10°C) dry place, out of direct sunlight. Well-brined and smoked joints of meat will probably keep for several days longer, especially if you have smoked them patiently at a low temperature (see page 94), and provided you store them at a cool and even temperature in dry surroundings. However, remember that neither the suggested weight losses (page 79) nor the curing and smoking times indicated in this book are intended as guides to safe *long*-term storage.

However well smoked they seem, do not attempt to store unchilled any minced-meat mixtures such as sausages, any offal except hearts, or any shellfish. Refrigerate or freeze them immediately after their brief maturing times.

If any food has not achieved its full weight loss, also refrigerate it at once. Even if it is meant to be eaten raw when fully processed, cook it and eat it as it stands – it will probably be good even if not fully smoked. Take no chances with it.

13
Hot Smoking

Hot smoking is the ancient form of smoke-cooking, and it still has the same two main functions. First it completes the smoking process quickly, while polishing up the food's flavour by giving it an extra 'skin' of smoke; second, it changes the flavour of some cold-smoked foods which do not taste their best raw.

Notice that food must have been salted and at least partly cold smoked first to qualify as being 'hot smoked'. Food which is treated *only* with hot smoke (page 9) has little if any smoked flavour under the surface and can only, honestly, be called smoke-cooked or smoke-roasted. It has merits of its own, but is not truly smoked food.

Some craftsmen say that food should be fully cold smoked before it is hot smoked, because that is the only way it gets a true smoked flavour right through and can be guaranteed safe; hot smoking, however mild the heat, partly seals the food's surface so that relatively little more smoke can penetrate it. However, provided the food is cold smoked well, for most of its total smoking time, and is hot smoked for a comparatively short time at the end, you should get the fully smoky flavour and also enough weight-loss to preserve it for the same length of time as if it had been completely cold smoked. No home-smoked product, whether hot smoked or cold smoked, should be kept for more than a few days unless – if suitable – you freeze it.

Hot-smoked food gives you benefits which make up for the extra processing. You get not only the subtle flavour of the cold-smoked food enriched by the surface flavour given by the hot smoke, but the quite different taste-experience of *cooked* smoked food. Try cold smoking and hot smoking mackerel fillets, as the Norwegians do, and then eat them both cold at the same meal; the difference is obvious. Hot smoking, in short, gives you a much wider choice of foods through flavour (and colour) variations.

101

Another benefit is that any hot-smoked food is ready to eat right after processing, either cold or hot, straight from the smoker, whereas a good many cold-smoked foods must be cooked afterwards in the kitchen.

HOTTING-UP THE SMOKE

The hot-smoking process consists simply of raising the heat in which you bathe the food to a temperature which, though usually lower than that used for any normal cooking, will nonetheless cook the food in time, making it edible without further processing. Both the time and the exact temperature depend on the type of food, the size and weight of the pieces and how long you have given them in cold smoke. As a very general guide, fish should be hot smoked at not more than 180°F/83.5°C, but meat and poultry put up with quite a lot more bullying. Lean flesh is likely, however, to become dry and leathery if the temperature goes over 200° – 220°F/93.5° – 108°C.

Some craftsmen use separate kilns or smokers for cold and hot smoking, which may save fuel if the cold-smoking space is large and the hot-smoking one is smaller. It is also convenient in some cases, for instance if you want to cold smoke a second batch while hot smoking the first. However, for most of us one dual-purpose smoker is the only practical choice.

It has certain advantages too. No smoked food should be allowed to cool to near room-temperature in the air and then be given relatively low heating as in most hot smoking; if by any chance it has not been fully salted or cold smoked enough, there could be at least a slight risk of bacterial infection when it is transferred from a cold-smoking to a hot-smoking kiln or smoker, especially if it has to be left lying around while the hot-smoking kiln heats up. Besides this, some foods are best hot smoked by raising the smoke temperature gradually from cold-smoking heat. That gives an even stronger case for not taking them out of the protective smoke-laden air to be processed further elsewhere. It is also a lot more work to take them from one smoker, trundle them elsewhere and re-hang them.

The way you raise the heat depends on the type of smoker and the fuel you use. In effect you must reverse the processes by which you kept the food cool when cold smoking it. Small hardwood logs can be added to a wood-chip and sawdust fire, for instance, or you may be able to add a gas-burner as a second heat source. The method does not matter provided you reach the required heat level quickly or slowly as your recipe requires, and can maintain that long enough to give the hot-smoked results you want. Times, like temperatures, are given in individual recipes later in this book.

One other point. A few fish products seem to come out best if hot smoked for a while and then given slightly *less* heat. To do this you will again have to reverse your fire-handling techniques, at least marginally, so allow for it when you first make the fire or set up a second heat source.

In the smoke

Raising the heat alters the quality of the smoke; it releases certain components of the fuel which the smoke then carries and deposits on the food. These, as well as the action of the heat, seal the food surface, giving mackerel fillets, for instance, a much deeper golden glow than cold-smoked products have, and an intenser smoky flavour.

Some fish, however, are much better if the hot-smoking time is kept very short. Giving them an attractively bronzed coat and full flavour then presents problems. Raising the heat would over-cook them, just as hot smoking them for too long does. The answer is simply to give them more smoke briefly. Unlike in cold smoking, when you aim to keep the flow of smoke even, you may need to increase the volume of smoke quite a lot for some hot-smoking recipes. The simplest way to do this is to add extra smoking fuel, usually sawdust; make sure that your fire is active enough to ignite the addition.

REPEAT PERFORMANCE

Although food for hot smoking is placed in the smoking chamber in exactly the same way as for cold smoking, the fire behaves quite differently. It is when hot smoking that you curse windy weather or broiling sun if you have an outdoor smoker, as gusts of smoke or scorching heat attack your eyeballs when you peer in to see whether you have created enough smoke and a fire that is hot enough but not too hot.

It is all worthwhile, however, when you take from the smoker your amber-gold herring, haddock or mackerel, chestnut or mahogany-coloured chicken, duck or game. As you hang them or lay them out to mature, pride in your creation will surface. You will, though, have more to boast about if you finish off the job properly.

Although you can, if you wish, eat hot-smoked foods straight from the smoker, they are best cold and need maturing, just as cold-smoked ones do, to bring out their full flavour. They are also more economical to serve cold, because they can be sliced more thinly. Follow exactly the same procedure as when drying-off food after brining or cold smoking.

Store the food in the same way too. Wrap the pieces closely in diamond aluminium foil (with extra pads of foil or newspaper round the bone ends of birds, chops or joints). Refrigerate or freeze. Label with an 'Eat by...' date whichever you do. It is as easy to be careless about leaving food uneaten when it is staring you in the face in the refrigerator as when it is out of sight in the freezer.

Almost all smoked foods freeze well, but hot-smoked items should be particularly carefully wrapped – both to prevent their strong flavours tainting other food, and to protect them from drying out.

14
Smoke-cooking

The principles of all kinds of smoke-cooking are described in Chapter 9. Here is a step-by-step guide to assembling a smoke-box and using it – first for smoke-cooking, then for cold smoking.

1 Wherever you decide to smoke, outdoors or indoors, make sure that the site is level, heatproof and reasonably free from draughts. Methylated spirit is generally used as the heating fuel, and remember that when hot it may spill over the top of its container and spread, burning, over sloping or uneven ground. So if out of doors, see that no inflammable material of any kind, twigs, dry grass, scraps of paper etc, is anywhere near it. Stand it on bare ground, a stone or brick patio floor or a path, out of the wind or protected by a small fire-break. Indoors, place it on a level fired-tile, stone or steel surface, such as a level draining board, and clear the area of any material which might ignite. Keep it out of draughts but make sure there is an open window near by to let smoke escape. Use only solid-fuel firelighters indoors as an extra precaution.

2 The smallest of the range of smoke-boxes illustrated (drawing 15) has one shallow fuel pan, the next largest has two, the next size up has two deep pans and the largest has six. Place the pan or pans where you want to use them, test-position the smoke-box on top, then remove it and assemble it beside the pans.

3 If your model has a loose base-plate, put it in place. Sprinkle the centre with the right quantity of smoking dust for the foods to be smoke-cooked (almost all smoke-boxes are supplied with an instruction manual which tells you this). Cover the baffle-plate with foil for easy cleaning, and place it on top of the dust. Place the lower rack (if more than one) on top of that.

4 Cover the rack with prepared pieces of food not more than 1½in/3.5cm thick; keep to the quantity recommended in the

maker's manual. Fish and meat can be smoke-cooked at the same time. They can be brined, partly brined, marinated or simply seasoned. If using more than one rack, place dryer items on the lower one, so that drippings from fattier items above will baste them.

5 Put an upper rack in place if used, and cover it with food. Put on the lid.

6 Fill deep pans with methylated spirit to within 1in/2.5cm of the top, shallow pans to within ½in/1cm of the top. Alternatively, use solid-fuel firelighters broken into two or three pieces each. Light with a taper, then position the closed smoke-box over the pans.

7 Leave the smoke-box well alone until the fuel has burned away. Then either remove the lid at once, *wearing thick gloves*, and take out the rack of food for eating hot, while mildly coloured and smoked; or leave the food to cool in the smoke-box, when it will acquire a deeper colour and flavour.

8 When the smoke-box has cooled completely, unwrap the foil on the baffle-plate, remove the base-plate and scrape off the burned smoking dust. Wash all parts except the fuel pans with detergent and hot water, but do not use abrasive on a non-stick inside coating. Dry in the open air and reassemble.

HOT-BOX COLD SMOKING

1 This process is much more akin to normal cold smoking, but the food is smoked under slight pressure, because the smoke outlet on the smoke-box is very small. The cold-smoke attachment (drawing 16) is used instead of any fuel pans. Place it on level heatproof ground where there is room for it to stand in front of one of the two largest Brooks smoke-boxes. It *must* be outdoors: *charcoal gives off fumes which can be lethal* in an enclosed space.

2 Place a solid-fuel firelighter, broken in half, at each end of the fire compartment in the cold-smoke attachment. Light them. When burning well, cover with a stack of charcoal.

3 When the charcoal is alight, cover with about half as much charcoal again, and spread the charcoal over the bottom of the fire compartment. Let it get well alight; this takes about three-quarters of an hour, given a slight breeze. It should be turning white underneath.

4 While the charcoal gets going, assemble the smoke-box as in

steps 3 – 5 of the 'Hot-box' smoke-cooking process already described, but without smoking or heating fuel. Raise the base-plate on the wooden blocks supplied with the cold-smoke attach-ment. Use only brined, dried-off pieces of food, all of the same type and thickness. Larger and somewhat thicker pieces can be processed than when smoke-cooking – say split small chickens or whole large mackerel.

5 Position the cold-smoke attachment so that its open end (oppo-site the fire compartment) rests about 1in/2.5cm inside the hole at the base of the smoke-box stand. Sprinkle the charcoal with 2 – 3 tablespoons of smoking dust, and fit on the lid of the fire compartment. Make sure that it fits tightly under the top edge of the hole in the smoke-box base.

6 Given a slight breeze, inspect and top up the smoking dust every 1½ hours, adding each time some of the hickory chips supplied with the kit. On a very still day, it may burn less fast and in fact need 'helping' with bellows or some other draught-producing mechanism after 3 – 4 hours. In a strong wind, the fuel may need topping-up more often.

7 Continue until the food has the smoky flavour and colour you want. The weight loss will probably not be as great as in normal cold smoking, so is not much help as a guide. Smoking times are also quicker. Although a matter of personal choice, and of the type of brine or pickle used, the following times are a general guide to smoke-box cold 'smoking' in light wind conditions:

salmon, side	8 – 10 hours
whole small fatty fish, about 12oz/340g	10 hours
skinned poultry joints or slightly smaller pieces of red meat	6 – 8 hours
very small birds (eg quail) or offal (organ meats)	2 – 4 hours

OVEN-ROASTED SMOKED MEATS

In a conventional oven, slow-roasting is a recognised alternative to the usual high-heat roasting. Temperatures used range between 325°F/160°C/Gas 3 and 350°F/180°C/Gas 4. More important, from your point of view, a meat thermometer gives an interior tempera-ture of 140°F/60°C for rare beef, 167°F/75°C for well-done beef, and 179°F/82°C for all other meat, except pork (186°F/86°C). Provided your roasting meat reaches these interior temperatures, there is no reason why you should not transfer it to a smoker preheated for hot-smoking for the last part of its cooking time; it will get a good smoked surface flavour, although the smoke will hardly penetrate it at all. Transfer it as quickly as possible, before it can cool, and adjust the cooking time as the temperature in the smoking chamber requires. Use an oven thermometer if possible, whether you know the temperature inside your smoking chamber or not. A drip-tray is also essential.

Do not attempt to give meat or poultry more than a short part of its normal cooking time in the smoke, say the last half-hour for a sizeable solid joint. Meat, especially, may get a hard leathery surface if smoke-cooked for too long. Generally, too, the food has not been brined, and if the smoking-chamber temperature is lower than 325°F/160°C, bacteria can develop in the centre of a partly roasted joint or chicken which may survive even full cooking. For this reason never smoke-cook stuffed meat or birds, even for a short time.

If you can preheat your smoking chamber accurately to 350°F/180°C or higher, you can cook small meat cuts, or poultry or game joints, in it for most or all of their cooking time if you want a 'manly' smoked flavour, provided you season and oil or grease them well first. Effectively you then use your smoker like a hot-box.

Some smoking authorities recommend smoke-roasting larger joints or whole birds in a hot-smoking temperature of between 200° and 225°F (93.5° and 106.5°C), to avoid surface hardening, for their entire cooking time, but in my view this is risky, especially when using commercially bred foods. A safer method sometimes recommended is to start smoke-roasting meat (or more often birds) in the smoker, but to complete the cooking in an ordinary oven with the food closely wrapped in foil to preserve its succulence, using a meat thermometer to make sure it is fully cooked through.

'KETTLE-ROASTED' SMOKED MEATS

Like hot-box smoke-cooking, 'kettle'-smoking can be used for unbrined, brined or marinated meat, poultry, fish and other foods, and you have a wider choice of products since whole joints or birds can be smoke-cooked.

1 Assemble your 'kettle', following the maker's instructions. Find a level heatproof site outdoors for it, protected from strong winds. It must be outdoors because of the risk of charcoal fumes.

2 If required, soak the wood chips or chunks in cold water for up to 1 hour, or as your instruction manual recommends.

3 Make a charcoal fire in the 'kettle', again following the manufacturer's instructions. Remember to open any vents on the 'kettle' while getting the fire going. Usually, it will take 30 – 40 minutes to get hot enough to start cooking.

4 Load the 'kettle' with prepared food which has been well oiled or greased. Insert a meat thermometer in a meat joint or bird. Put on thick oven gloves, and close the vents. Put on the lid.

5 Either at once or later, depending on the type of food and the strength of smoked flavour you want, add the smoking fuel. If you prefer, you can almost fully roast or barbecue-cook the food without smoke, basting it from time to time by lifting the lid, or opening a fire-door if your smoke cooker has one, and only add the smoking fuel towards the end. You can however add the fuel right away if you prefer, for flavouring small pieces of food or for a sturdy 'hunter's meat' taste. Shake excess moisture off the smoking fuel if soaked, then add it to the fire.

Continue basting as required until the food is done.

6 When the food is ready, either eat it right away (small items such as fish fillets, steaks or a chicken); or take it out of the smoke-cooker and let it 'rest', covered with a warm, dry cloth for 10 – 20 minutes, then carve it and eat it hot (sizeable joints and large birds such as turkey); or cool it quickly, preferably over ice, then refrigerate it, wrapped (not too tightly), for 24 hours to bring out and mellow the smoked flavour, then eat cold or reheat if appropriate (any food).

Cooking times in a 'kettle' smoker

Food	Weight	Approx Cooking Time	Temp on Meat Thermometer
Beef (any roasting cut or brisket)	3 – 4lb/1.5 – 2kg	4 – 5 hours	140°F/60°C
Lamb (any roasting cut)	5 – 7lb/2.5 – 3kg	5 – 6 hours	160°F/71°C
Venison (any roasting cut)	7 – 9lb/3 – 4kg	6 – 8 hours	160° – 170°F/71° – 77°C

Pork roasting cuts	3 – 4lb/1.5 – 2kg	5 – 6 hours	170°F/77°C
Pork chops	In the piece to fit cooker grill	2 – 3 hours	until meat pulls away from bone
Spare ribs (beef)	"	3 – 4 hours	"
(pork)	"	4 – 6 hours	"
Ham, whole raw	10 – 18lb/4.5 – 8kg	10 – 12 hours	170°F/77°C
Ham, whole cooked	10 – 14lb/4.5 – 6.5kg	3 – 4 hours	160°F/71°C
Chicken, split or joints	1 – 4 broilers (fryers)	3 – 4 hours	180°F/82.5°C
Chicken, whole	1 – 4 broilers (fryers)	4 – 5 hours	"
Chicken, roasting	1 × 4 – 5lb/2 – 2.5kg	5 – 6 hours	185°F/85°C
Turkey, unstuffed	8 – 12lb/3.5 – 5.5kg	7 – 8 hours	"
	12 – 18lb/5.5 – 8kg	9 – 10 hours	"
Duck, unstuffed	3 – 5lb/1.5 – 2.5kg	4 – 6 hours	185°F/85°C
Goose, unstuffed	8 – 10lb/3.5 – 4.5kg	7 – 8 hours	"
Fish, small whole, fillets or steaks	–	1½ – 3 hours	until flesh flakes with fork
whole larger	3 – 6lb/1.5 – 3kg	3 – 4 hours	"
Shellfish, eg large prawns (shrimps)	–	1 hour	until firm and pink (if prawns)

REHEATS

All hot-smoked and smoke-cooked foods can be reheated or used to make cooked dishes like fresh pre-cooked or delicatessen smoked products. See the recipes in Chapter 18.

COOKED COLD-SMOKED FOODS

Cold-smoked foods have *not* been cooked, either in a conventional smoker or in a hot-box with a cold-smoke attachment. Some can

110

be eaten uncooked after being matured; smoked salmon is the best known example. Some other fish such as commercially smoked kipper fillets (kippered herring) can be eaten uncooked, although in fact these are almost always lightly cooked by being dipped in boiling water for a few minutes. Some other foods definitely need further cooking to make them pleasant to eat; raw bacon, for instance, is not a gourmet dish (although commercially smoked raw Westphalian and Parma ham are).

Cold-smoked meats and poultry which need further cooking must have more than merely gentle cooking heat. For instance, grill or fry sausages, or bake them at not less than 350°F/180°C/Gas 4, or boil them for long enough to cook them right through. Even quite heavily cured foods are best cooked at a high temperature, especially if soaked to leach out some of their salt, eg a country-style bacon joint must be boiled and/or baked like a fresh one.

Don't take a chance with any home-smoked foods. Cook quickly and thoroughly any cold-smoked food which you want to eat hot, whether it needs it or you do it just for its flavour.

MAXIMUM STORAGE TIMES FOR SMOKE-COOKED FOODS

Fish, non-fatty	24 hours
Fish, fatty	"
Shellfish	12 hours
Butcher's meats	3 days
Chicken	3 days
Duck or game	2 days
Liver, kidney etc	24 hours
Sausages	2 days
Cheese	2 weeks
Eggs	3 days
Fruit, vegetables	2 – 3 days

These times are for foil-wrapped refrigerated foods. After these times, foods begin to dry out and lose flavour.

15
Good Foods to Smoke

The original idea behind smoking food was to preserve what could not be eaten right away and would go bad otherwise – fatty foods, especially. In earlier times meat and fish rich in fat went rancid before they could be properly air-dried. Besides this, they tasted better after being salted and smoked than very lean foods. So when fishermen brought home more fish than the village could eat, the limited space for smoking was mostly used for oily, well-flavoured common fish such as herring, mackerel and salmon in northern Europe, and white coarse fish were usually salted or pickled in vinegar; in more southern lands with less fuel but more sunshine, such fish were often sun- and air-dried until as hard as boards. (Anyone who has stood on an African river-bank and smelled the fish drying will know one reason why salting and smoking became a popular alternative.) When hunters made a good killing, or domestic beasts and poultry were killed, no part was wasted. If the animals could not be fed in winter, at least they could feed man. Cattle, being lean and scraggy, were usually just dry salted or 'powdered' as it was called for rich men's tables. Pigs, being fatty, became long-smoked bacon and hams for unending winter meals for everyone else.

MEAT, FISH AND BIRDS

With some additions, the foods that proved best when smoked in the past are the ones we smoke today. They comprise, on the whole, the fattier fish and a few common round white fish such as haddock, whiting and cod. These white fish are usually only lightly processed. Virtually no flat fish are included, but eels are, being fatty. The fleshier shellfish, such as oysters, mussels and clams, smoke best.

In the same way, the more solid offals such as kidneys, hearts, tongues and liver (which looks dreadful and tastes delicious), smoke well, whereas brains and sweetbreads do not. Most very lean beef, especially if tough, is still best simply pickled and boiled (although this is a subjective view). Pig meats, from bacon to burgers, are still the prime favourites for smoking among butcher's meats.

North Americans have made smoked turkey a popular party feature which is now becoming known in Britain and elsewhere. Smoked turkey sausages must be tried! The European taste for other smoked poultry is only just beginning to develop in Britain – far too slowly, for there are few foods more luxuriously splendid than smoked goose or duck, and the humble chicken takes on a new and succulent dimension.

As a way of handling elderly game birds and furred game, smoking is unrivalled. Those country-dwellers in the northern hemisphere who by the end of the shooting season are tired of 'wild meat' will probably find that smoking their pheasant or partridge is rewarding, and keen hunters will find it a good way to process venison, just as it was in ancient times. In Britain, experts say red deer or roebuck meat is best; fallow-deer meat is a luxury just plainly roasted.

The British brown or blue hare (jack rabbit, Arctic hare) is not ideal smoking meat, being dryish and strongly flavoured already, but it can be smoked lightly, with care, to vary its flavour. Wild rabbit is better for smoking, being smaller, fleshier and less strongly flavoured.

Farmed or tame rabbit, although bred originally from wild rabbit, seems more like a different species: its flesh is paler and softer, and the flavour is mild; it can be treated exactly like chicken. In Britain, the meat is widely available fresh or frozen as skinned joints, which are excellent when smoke-cooked (blocks of frozen boneless rabbit meat are not suitable).

CHEESE, BURGERS, EGGS, PLANT FOODS, NUTS AND SALT

Various foods besides flesh foods can be smoked as delicacies. Cheese is one. Processed quite differently from commercial smoked cheeses, it responds well to smoke-cooking, gaining a slightly toasted-cheese flavour. Hard-pressed Cheddar-type cheeses are less satisfactory than less mature, more 'plastic' cheeses which contain more moisture; a lot of fat melts out of hard cheese, leaving the paste condensed and 'flannelly'. Blue cheeses should *not* be smoke-cooked; they taste harsh and bitter. Nor should any cream cheese, or any cheese containing peppers or pineapple. Blended English cheeses such as Rutland or Cotswold can be used, but avoid using very spicy or garlicky cheeses. Plain processed cheese – *without* additions such as chopped peppers – is excellent when smoke-cooked and cut into cubes for cocktail snacks, or sliced for sandwiches.

Home-made meaty burgers or sausages are also a good and unusual lunch-box item, either smoked or smoke-cooked, provided they are thoroughly processed to avoid any risk of bacterial infection (page 11).

Smoked hard-boiled eggs are another unusual product. They are not always brined first, and are best gently cold smoked until amber-gold. They can be used as a 'starter', in salads, a lunch-box or picnic or as a garnish for any cold fish or meat platter.

Smoked vegetables and fruits may sound a foolish idea, but in fact bits of onion and other vegetables find their way into a lot of smoked sausage mixtures. On the whole, watery vegetables are not suitable, nor are juicy fruits which are very acid. Skip, therefore, cucumbers, peppers and fruits such as oranges or plums. In a 'hot-box', try smoke-cooking well-seasoned (but not brined) onion rings, mushrooms or apple rings, either sprinkled with dripping or on the baffle-plate under fattier foods such as sausages, which will baste them during cooking. They make a good addition to a hot picnic meal.

Most kinds of shelled nuts can be lightly cold smoked as tasty cocktail snacks. They should be salted after smoking, not before.

Some craftsmen smoke their own salt on foil trays, to augment the smoked flavour of other foods.

You will find directions for preparing and smoking all suitable types of food in the next two chapters. There are also, of course, many hundreds of other specialities; the range of French, Italian, German and other smoked sausages, each processed differently, would fill a book in itself; so would the Scandinavian smoked fish products, or the various British and American hams. The recipes given in this book will whet your appetite, so that as you become experienced you can forage further for yourself.

SUITABLE FOODS TO SMOKE

Fish and shellfish

Bluefish	Haddock	Scallops
Char	Herring	Shad
Clams	Mackerel	Smelts
Cod	Mussels	Sprats
Cod's roe	Octopus	Sturgeon
Conger eel	Oysters	Swordfish
Dublin Bay prawns	Pilchards (fresh)	Trout (all kinds)
(jumbo prawns)	Prawns	Tuna
Eel	Salmon	Whitefish
Grayling	Salmon–trout	Whiting
Grey mullet	Sardines (fresh)	

Butcher's, game and offal (organ) meats

Beef	Mutton
Heart – ox (beef), calf's, pig's, lamb's	Pork
Kidneys – ox (beef), pig's	Rabbit (wild and farmed)
Lamb	Tongue (fresh – ox (beef), calf's, pig's)
Liver – ox (beef), pig's, poultry, game	(Veal is not suitable)
	Venison

Birds

Chicken (all sizes up to 4lb/1.8kg dressed weight for smoking whole)	Quail
	Partridge
	Pheasant
Domestic duck (not more than 4lb/1.8kg dressed weight for smoking whole)	Turkey (not more than 10lb/ 5.5kg dressed weight for smoking whole)
Goose	Wild duck (all types if not too fishy)
Grouse (old birds)	
Guineafowl	

Other products

Almonds	Hazelnuts
Apple rings	Mushrooms
Brazil nuts	Onion rings
Cheese, semi-hard, yielding and processed	Peanuts
Eggs, hard-boiled	Salt
	Sunflower seeds

CHOOSING THE RIGHT QUALITY

The foods you smoke need not be rare, luxurious products. There is a lot to be said for using some everyday ones which usually taste dull or are coarse in texture, because pickling and smoking can tenderise and re-flavour them, making them beguilingly different. Any food you smoke must however be in peak condition for its type. Watch for these points:

Fish must be absolutely fresh. Stale fish will still taste poor, be flabby, and may disintegrate in smoking. It may even go off during drawn-out processing. Avoid white (non-fatty) fish with soft flesh, small bony white fish and most flat fish. They are usually not worth the trouble of processing. Choose fairly large eels at least 2in/5cm in diameter; smaller ones shrivel.

Shellfish must be processed straight from the sea, or from the freezer as soon as thawed.

Meat should come from animals in good condition before slaughter, and beef and winter lamb especially must have been well conditioned (hung to mature) professionally. If you get home-killed venison, you will of course have to hang and brine it yourself to the degree of gamyness you prefer, after it is butchered (see page 125).

Bulk buying by a family or group of friends is often a sensible way to get good meat cheaply, by buying either a whole or split carcass (or a large part of a beef one) or a package of assorted or similar cuts. If you have a smoker, these are convenient ways to get varied cuts to smoke especially when you are still experimenting, or to get similar ones which are easy to brine together. You may also find it more practical to buy in bulk for the freezer if you can smoke some cuts to vary the flavour. Unappealing 'bits' such as trimmings need not be wasted either, if minced and smoked for sausages and pâtés.

However you buy it, choose good-quality, moderately fatty beef; the cut surfaces will be dull red. A lamb carcass should be under 40lb/18kg in weight or it will be too fatty; look for fleshy shoulders, thick short legs and good visible pinkish or light red lean meat, depending on age. Choose meat from a mutton carcass around 50lb/23kg in weight, conditioned for at least a week if possible. The meat should be dull red, with firm creamy fat. Choose good-quality pork to avoid over-fatty meat; the kidney should be visible. Pork from young porkers is bland and less suitable for smoking than heavier, slightly older pig-meat; in Britain, this comes from fast-fattened pigs or from under-grade or surplus bacon pigs, and is more flavoursome than porker meat. The meat should be light pink with firm white fat.

Any good general cookery book describes what the various conventional meat cuts should look like and weigh, and their quality. In general, avoid meat with a lot of cartilage or gristle, or wads of fat.

Minced meats, eg for sausages, must be prepared as soon as the meat has been butchered, using scrupulously clean scalded tools. It must then be processed without delay. Any minced mixture, however well spiced, is a better-than-average breeding ground for bacteria. It is warm after being minced, and a lot of cut meat surface is exposed to air. The more finely it is minced, the bigger the risk.

Poultry should be used as soon as it has been plucked and cooled after slaughter, or straight from the freezer once thawed: commercially bred and frozen poultry in particular!

Game birds should be hung *almost* to the degree you would like to eat them when roasted fresh. Some people like a gamy flavour, others don't. Water-birds with a strongly fishy flavour should not be smoked.

Venison (British red deer or roebuck) should ideally be young, with small smooth clefts in the hooves. In practice, you have to trust the supplier from whom you buy the meat (usually ready-hung), or accept what the hunter brings home. The same goes for home-killed wild rabbit, although if buying one, you should try to choose a young rabbit, wild or tame; it is best at about 4 months old with thick foot joints, smooth claws and tender ears which tear easily.

Liver and kidneys whether from meat, poultry or game, should be very fresh.

Eggs are easier to shell if not fresh from the nest. (For most city-dwellers, nest-fresh eggs are such a treat it's a shame not to eat them freshly boiled or poached anyway.) Use eggs about a week old for smoking. Do not use long-chilled or stale eggs, because the yolks will tend to be off-centre and surrounded by a greyish ring after hard-boiling.

Cheeses should be at their peak of condition. Do not use any cheese which is dry and cracked, or 'sweating'. Smoking will not retrieve any cheese which is pungently overripe. Remember (pages 113–14) that mature hard cheeses are not suitable; nor is any blue cheese or cream or Brie-style quick-ripening cheese or a blended cheese containing strong garlic, peppers or pineapple.

16
Preparing the Food

The tools needed are suggested on pages 68–69. Whether you set aside a special area for preparing foods for smoking of course depends on how much smoking you intend to do, and of which foods. But as far as possible, prepare fish and meat, meat products and other foods in separate areas or at different times. Scrupulous cleanliness is essential. Keep separate tools for fish, and do not use them for other things. Fishy aromas cling even after a wash!

Decide how you will hang fish, poultry, meat joints, etc, for drying and smoking; then, when preparing them, leave in place supporting bones or a tapered piece of flesh which will hold a hook or loop of string securely. Prepare food fully before salting or brining, but only insert hooks, sticks, etc, after it.

FISH

Keep your fingers well rubbed with salt while preparing fish: you will be able to hold it more firmly.

Scaling
Fins should be removed first, and the coarse scales on fish such as herring, sea bream and red mullet. Lay the fish on soft kitchen paper. Cut off the fins with sharp scissors. Hold the fish by the tail, and scrape both sides with the back of a knife, working towards the head. Rinse or wipe off loose scales occasionally.

Gutting
Very small fish such as small fresh sardines and sprats (and herring smoked for the special product called bloaters) can be processed whole, but almost all other fish need gutting, if it has not been done before you bought them. Most round fish are gutted by making a slit with a sharp knife along the length of the belly from

the bony shoulder plates to the vent; herring have hardly any 'innards' except when full of roe, and usually only need a short slit, from the ear-bones behind the gills along the belly, or the guts can be squeezed out from the head end if beheading the fish. Slit eels to below the vent, to take out the kidney etc. Open up the fish (or take off a herring's head) and extract the guts gently, keeping any hard or soft roe intact if you want it. Discard the rest (including eel kidney). Take out the blood vessel at the back of the cavity of most fish (eg salmon, mackerel) by breaking the membrane over it and scraping it clean. Squeeze out any visible veins in the belly walls of salmon, and scrape or peel off black skin lining the belly walls of some white fish. Rinse the cavity and pat dry.

Most fish are smoked with skin on, but have their heads removed before brining and smoking. Remove the eyes if you leave the head on. Rinse again.

Splitting

The commonest way to split round fish is to extend the slit made for gutting the fish down to the tail. Then, with the fish on its back, slit uppermost, cut through the ribs and flesh close to one side of the spine but without cutting through the back skin. (The head can be split as well, but is more often removed, leaving the ear-bones to support a hook or string for hanging the fish.) Press on the fish to open it flat. Take out the spine if you wish, except for a short piece at the tail end if you intend to hang the fish by the tail.

To remove the spine, turn the fish over, skin-side up, press on the spine all the way down, then turn the fish over again, and lift up the spine with a knife point. Snip it at each end, and remove it. Remove the remaining ribs if you wish by sliding the knife blade under them and cutting them free with as little flesh as possible.

Filleting

A round fish only yields 2 fillets, one from each side (flat fish yield 4). To fillet round fish, lay the gutted fish on its side. Make a half-moon cut just below the head and gills. Insert a knife point in the back of the fish at the top end of the cut, behind the head, and cut right along the spine to the tail. Then grasp the head in your left hand. Holding the knife flat and pressed against the spine and rib bones, slice off the whole side of the fish on top of the spine,

120

peeling it back from the half-moon cut as you do so. Turn the fish over and remove the second side in the same way. Rinse and remove loose bones.

Before salting, make small cuts through the flesh close to the head end of a split or filleted fish if you are going to hang the fish on a string or stick to dry and smoke it (see below).

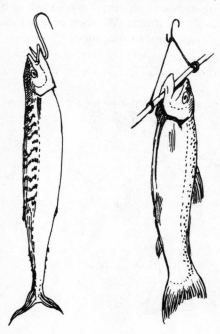

24, 25 Mackerel on hook and trout on rod

Hanging fish after curing

Smallish whole fish with heads on are sometimes hung by an S-shaped hook or stick passed through the throat (drawings 24, 25). The free end of the hook is then hung over a rod in the smoker, or hooked through the wire mesh of a rack. A stick is hung from a hook by a cord, then hung in the smoker in the same way.

Another method is to make an incision in each side of the fish at the head end, and to thread a wooden stick through the holes to hold the fish open and flat.

Small fish such as trout and mackerel for serving whole, and whole herring smoked as buckling, can also be skewered on a stick, run through the eye-sockets so as not to spoil the look of the smoked fish. They may also be speared on a stick through or about ¾in/1.8cm below the gills. In all these cases, a loop of cord or string is attached to the stick at each end, and is used as a hanger. Eels can be hung on hooks like small whole fish or be skewered on a stick run through the throat. Wooden cocktail picks are used to hold the belly cavity open to the smoke.

26, 27 Small fish on rod, and trout on rod through gills

If split fish are hung up by a loop of cord hung round the tail, also thread a stick through the broad end to keep them open.

Hanging by a string threaded through cuts at the head end is the traditional way of hanging salmon sides and other filleted fish. An incision similar to that for a stick is made, and a string is threaded through each side, with enough slack to form a loop above the fish. A thin stick is often used to skewer the fish open as well.

122

Laying on racks

Very small whole or split fish can be laid on racks (and must be for 'hot-box' smoking). The only disadvantage is that they show the impress of the wire mesh afterwards.

Cod's roes need special care because the very thin skin breaks easily. Rinse them gently under cold water before salting them lightly for a short time. Hang them in a muslin bag or piece of open-weave cheesecloth. Smoke or smoke-cook them on racks or on muslin or heavily perforated foil, and turn them over during smoking.

Oiling

Fish should not need any seasoning after brining or pickling, but most white, non-fatty fish and some others should be brushed with oil at this stage.

SHELLFISH

Prawns

Take off the heads. Peel if you wish. Wash and drain thoroughly. Soak unpeeled prawns in 40 per cent salt solution for 30 minutes; then boil them in the brine or in fresh water for 30 minutes. Dry for 2 hours, turning the pile over from time to time.

Peeled prawns can just be boiled for 3 – 4 minutes in the brine. They should then be dried on oiled mesh trays.

Mussels

Check over the unopened shellfish carefully and discard any open ones, or mussels which float when you scrub them. Clean and scrub thoroughly as for normal cooking. Put into fast-boiling water for 2 – 3 minutes until their shells open. Brine for 5 minutes in a 50 per cent brine solution.

Oysters

Check over and scrub oysters like mussels. Steam them in one layer, deep side down, until the shells open. Add the liquor to a 50 per cent brine. Cut the oysters out of the shells, and brine for 15 minutes. Oil well.

MEAT JOINTS AND PIECES

If you buy butcher's meat in bulk you may be faced with a very large piece of meat or a whole or split smaller carcass. Contract with a professional butcher to cope with beef or any frozen meat for you. Butchering beef requires more massive tools than you will need for any other food processing, and greater strength. Frozen meat must be butchered while still chilled. (A forequarter of beef is usually cut into seven parts: fore-rib, brisket, thick ribs, sticking, clod and shin. The hindquarter is cut into the top-piece (haunch), rump and loin and flank. The top-piece is then cut into conventional roasting and braising joints and pieces for mincing.)

After splitting, a side of lamb or mutton should be divided in half before jointing, just above the last rib, which is left on the hindquarter. A side of English pork is cut up in different ways in various parts of the country, depending on what the meat will be used for, but generally the heavier bacon pigs most useful for smoking are cut into four parts: the head or half-head (don't discard this); the blade bone with the forehock, knuckle and foot, equivalent to the shoulder in lamb (the forehock, etc, is called a hand); the main carcass, consisting of the English spare rib (equivalent to the best neck in lamb), the loin and chump; and the leg, cut square across the pelvis just above the tail. Although many local British butchers may have other ideas about how a side of pork should be cut, these will be convenient pieces to divide for home curing and smoking.

Trimming joints

Even if you buy assorted ready-prepared cuts of butcher's meats, you may still want to divide or trim them to the sizes and weights you want, so here are some notes on how to set about it.

1 Find a book or chart with diagrams showing how the conventional joints are cut, and where the bone joints are on the skeleton. A large general cookbook or cookery dictionary will often contain one, or in Britain a chart can be obtained free from an organisation such as British Meat (see page 173). The diagrams will not include a venison (deer) carcass, but will give you a shrewd idea of where its bone joints are.

2 Make sure that your knives are really sharp before you start

cutting. Hone (steel) them yourself, or ask a butcher to do it. Don't use a high-speed grinder; it spoils the blades.

3 Remove excess fat, any skin or membrane, and offal such as a lamb's kidney. Then cut steadily through the meat with a slight sawing motion, keeping your free hand well out of the way; either hold a bone, or hold the meat steady with a fork. A leather guard around your free wrist is advisable. Cut up all meat in the same way, whether dividing a side into parts, cutting into conventional joints or cutting into smaller pieces of equal size and weight.

Venison

Venison (deer-meat) must be processed promptly, especially if home-killed, as it deteriorates quickly. A home-killed venison carcass must be split and the soft white spinal cord removed, then be skinned and divided into the haunches (chump, rump and top of leg), loins, saddle (just above the loin) and shoulders for hanging. The remaining pieces are tough and should be marinated at once for up to 48 hours, then be minced for pies, sausages or pâtés.

Test that the meat is fresh by running a skewer into the rump as far as the bone. Wash well if at all smelly. Cut any thick fat off the meat pieces, dry thoroughly with a floured cloth, then rub with ground ginger. Wrap in muslin, including a few fresh bay leaves, and hang in a cool place. The gamy flavour will continue to develop while the meat cures, so do not over-hang. Shoulder and loin usually have too thin a flesh layer to smoke well; they are best roasted fresh or cooked as loin chops. Saddle and haunch are handsome roasting cuts, but a haunch is too large for most families: divide it into three or four pieces for roasting or for pickling and smoking. A saddle can be pickled and smoked if the thin layer of flesh is not overprocessed. Use the pickle for Furred Game on page 93, and the processing recipe on page 138.

Rabbit

A wild home-killed British rabbit should be paunched while still warm if possible, and cleaned with care, removing every scrap of intestine. Check that the liver is not discoloured or messy and that the cavity does not smell rank. Rinse the cavity well, and hang the rabbit by the hind legs for 24 hours – or less in warm weather. Skin the rabbit and joint it. Take off the head, neck, shoulders and forelegs in one piece by cutting through the spine and ribs just behind the shoulders; they are not worth smoking. Take off the hind legs and thighs in one piece each. Leave the hindquarters and saddle in one piece. Rinse well in salt water. Brine like salmon (page 91), using 1½lb/750g salt and 4oz/100g sugar, and substituting ½tsp/2.5ml dried mixed herbs for the onion salt and lemon juice. Leave in the brine for 10 – 12 hours in a cool place, then drain. Hang and dry off, then cold smoke at 80°F/26.5°C for 12 hours. Oil, and hot smoke at 180°F/82.5°C for 1 – 1½ hours until tender.

Tame rabbit can be treated in the same way, or like chicken (see below).

Organ, offal or variety meats
Prepare hearts, tongues, liver and kidneys before curing exactly as you would for ordinary cooking. Remove any tubes, excess fat, covering membrane, etc, from hearts, and wash out the cavities to remove blood clots. Trim the root of a tongue, removing tubes, gristle and sinews. Prick the skin to let salt penetrate. Leave livers whole, but snip out any tubes or membranes. Skin kidneys, halve and core them, then skewer with small pointed sticks or cocktail picks to hold them open during curing and smoking.

Small pieces
Cure miscellaneous pieces of meat which you want to use for smoked kebabs, pies, sausages, burgers or meatballs before cutting them up. (In a good many mixed-meat sausage recipes, the beef or other meat used with pork is cured, but the pork itself is not.)

For preparing minced-meat mixtures for sausages, etc, after curing, see page 140.

SPICING AND OILING MEAT

In the old days, dry-salted or plainly brined hams and other meats were rubbed with a spice or herb mixture during drying off and from time to time during the long intermittent cold-smoking process. It kept the flies off and varied the flavour of the meat.

Although most flavoured brines and pickles are well spiced, you may still like to give meats some extra flavouring before smoking if you have dry salted them or have only pickled them for a short time. Here is a basic dry-spicing mixture which can be stored in an airtight jar.

Dry spicing mixture

1tbsp onion powder	½ – 1tsp dry mustard
1tbsp garlic powder	1 – 3tbsp finely ground black pepper
1tsp ground allspice	1 – 3tbsp ground white pepper
1tsp ground mace or grated nutmeg	

Use freshly bought spices. Sift them together, then store for at least 48 hours before use. Vary the mixture to suit your taste or the flavour of the meat. Use hot paprika, for instance, instead of the allspice, mace and mustard. Ground cumin is another alternative for one of the spices.

Dust the meat liberally with the spicing mixture during or after drying off. The meat must be fairly dry or the spicing mixture may set like dried mud and prevent smoke penetration. (Apply to livers while still slightly moist.) Alternatively, rub the seasoning on the meat after cold smoking if the meat will be hot smoked.

Oiling

Lean meat usually needs oiling, either after drying off or between cold and hot smoking. Kettle smoked meat should be basted during cooking.

HANGING MEAT, SAUSAGES, ETC

Meat is usually easier to hang than fish, because the flesh is more solid. Pierce it with a hook, or thread a loop of string through it, and hang it up without fear of it dropping off. A leg or shoulder joint may have a knobbly projecting end of bone round which a string can be tied, and if you don't want to make a hole in boneless meat, you may be able to tie a loop of string round one end as in drawing 22. To hang a round or square piece of meat without projecting bone, stick a meat skewer firmly into each side and thread a loop of string through the holes in the rounded skewer heads; the holes made by the skewers will hardly show. This is a good way to hang an ox-heart (beef heart).

Stick a hook firmly through the root of a tongue.

To hang skewered kidneys, attach a string loop to the skewer on each side. Livers, however, must be laid on well-oiled perforated foil and smoked on racks; they will probably need turning over during smoking, so try to place them where you can get at them fairly easily.

Sausages are easy to hang if you do not separate links before smoking. Leave a short length of casing at the end of a string if you make your own sausages and either tie a looped string round it or (if slippery) put a small hook through it. Buy sausages in a string rather than a package, and tie a looped string between the end link and the next. Never stick a hook through a sausage.

BIRDS

Modern mass-farmed chickens and turkeys are the cheapest and most widely available meats to smoke, are easy to experiment on and rewarding to process – whole, split or as pieces – to vary their natural flavour. They can be smoked at home in three different ways: by hot smoking, by 'kettle' smoke-cooking, and (in pieces) by smoke-cooking in a 'hot-box'; to vary their flavours, they can be spiced in a dozen different styles.

There are only two 'don'ts', and they apply to any bird, tame or wild: *don't* stuff it, and *don't* rely just on cold smoking it. Salmonella bacteria can breed wantonly in a chopped or shredded mixture already warmed by processing; tucked safely in the moist warm cavity of the bird, gradually getting warmer, but never hot, they couldn't be happier. Any table bird, whether mass-farmed, free-range farmyard or wild, is a fertile bacterial host after death, whether stuffed or not; so lingering warmth, without sudden killing heat at the end, is out.

All table birds are prepared for smoking in much the same way, and on the whole they are easier to handle than meat. Land game birds (heath and moor game) may need hanging first, but otherwise only the brining and smoking times need be varied, to suit each bird's size, fattiness and natural flavour.

Grouse, pheasant and partridge in season are almost the only game birds smoked in Britain. (The seasons when they may be shot are strictly defined by law.) They should be hung by the necks, unplucked and undrawn, in a cool dark airy place, free from flies, to develop flavour; otherwise a pheasant tastes much like a chicken. However, for smoking, they must not be reeking high because the smoked flavour will be peculiar. As soon as the tail feathers move easily, the birds should be plucked, singed and drawn.

Plucking

All birds except wild water birds are plucked in the same way. If possible, pluck a home-killed chicken or other poultry bird while still warm. Dampen the feathers. Take them out, removing the wing and tail feathers first. Then singe the bird over a flame to remove the down, and rub it with a warm cloth to remove stubble and draw out the quills. Pluck these out. Cut part-way through the legs just below the drumsticks, without cutting the tendons; bend the legs in turn over the table edge to expose the tendons, then pull off the feet with the tendons. Cut off the head.

Drawing

Make a short upward cut from the vent, put in your hand or two fingers (depending on the size of the bird) and loosen the 'innards' all round the wall of the cavity. Draw them out, pick up the liver and heart (and gizzard if you want it), and carefully snip the greenish gall-bladder sac away from the liver over a cup. Discard it. Put the liver and heart aside and discard the rest. Rinse the bird inside (and your hands), then remove any thick wads of fat round the inside of the vent and neck of mass-farmed poultry in particular. (This fat is excellent if rendered down for ordinary cooking.) Rinse again thoroughly.

Prick the bird well all over, through the skin and down into the flesh especially the thick parts. Ducks need extra close-set deep pricks all over because of their thick fatty skin-layer.

Any bird which you will salt and smoke whole is now ready for brining.

Splitting

Large birds are usually more convenient to smoke if split in half. A whole large turkey with its thick compact flesh and heavy carcass takes a long time to brine and smoke and will be difficult to smoke safely and tastily in a small smoker. (It is usually 'kettle'-smoked if whole.)

The most important part of splitting any bird is to cut through the breast bone, shaving the central projecting ridge all the way along. The easiest way to split small and medium-sized birds is to up-end the bird on its neck end, grasp one leg in your left hand and cut straight downward between the legs, through the wish-bone and along the centre line of the breast and the spine.

A turkey or large duck with its rigid breast-bone may be cumbersome or difficult to split in this way with a knife, and may need attacking, on end or breast-side-up, with a light cleaver.

To quarter a bird, split it first, then cut each half into two more or less equal portions through the lower ribs.

Jointing

If a bird is to be jointed for smoke-cooking, stretch out each leg in turn and move it to locate the ball and socket joint at the pelvis. Cut through it and remove the leg. Deal with wings in the same way, taking them off close to the joint. Wings from small poultry and game birds are usually discarded or used for stock-making. Some people take off the wings together with the lower fillet of breast meat on each side, remove the pinion ends of the wings at the first joint, and smoke-cook the wings as chicken portions.

If you do not use the wings, take off the whole breast of the bird in one piece, by cutting horizontally through the vent slit, the flesh just above the pelvis, and the ribs, to the neck end. The spine and lower carcass has some flesh on it, but not enough to serve, so it is best used for stock. The breast can be split or smoke-cooked whole, depending on size. Turkey legs should be divided into thigh and drumstick portions; the legs of other substantial birds can also be divided, but may be more convenient to hang from the drumstick end as single joints if you have a sizeable smoker. Divide them for 'hot-box' smoke-cooking.

28 Chicken on rod

Hanging birds

The best way to hang most whole birds is to loop a string under the wings, as shown in drawing 21. This exposes the maximum skin area and the cavity to the air for drying, and to the smoke later.

For showy serving, a bird can be spitted on a pointed stick hung from a looped string in the smoker. Extend the legs, skewering them if required to hold them parallel, slightly apart. Tuck the wings into the sides with the pinions bent underneath the bird (drawing 28).

When 'kettle'-smoking, simply lay a whole bird on the smoking grill. Lay pieces or joints on the food carrier of a smoke-box in the same way.

Dry off thoroughly before smoking according to individual recipes.

OTHER PRODUCTS

Cheeses

Use block rather than round cheeses if possible – it saves space, especially in a 'hot-box' smoker. Remove any rind or wax coating. Cut cheese into 4 – 8oz/100 – 225g blocks not more than 2in/5cm thick. Slice horizontally like sandwiches if you wish, and sprinkle cut sides with any chopped fresh herbs or spices which suit the flavour of the cheese. Re-shape. Place in perforated foil pans with about ¼in/5mm space all round. Place a sprig of the fresh herb or a sprinkling of the spice (if used) on top for identification.

Grated leftover cheese can be 'hot-box' smoke-cooked, either plain or mixed with chopped herbs. Press well down in foil pans. After smoke-cooking, mop off any free fat. The cheese should have a golden crust and be solidified.

Shelled hard-boiled eggs

These will show the impress of the mesh if laid on racks. If placed in a wooden egg rack, they will have a ring of unsmoked pallor around them. Alternatively, spear them on wooden cocktail picks at the broad end, the picks then being put through the mesh of a rack in the smoker so that the eggs stand upright on the rack and only one end touches the mesh.

Put shelled eggs into 70 per cent brine, for 15 minutes, if you wish, then cold smoke until golden-amber, or with other foods until convenient.

131

Nuts
Must be shelled, blanched and skinned. Dry well, then scatter thinly in perforated foil pans. Cold smoke until nuts have a flavour you like (anything from 3 – 8 hours) or with other foods until convenient.

Apple, mushroom and onion rings
Peel apples, take off mushroom stems, skin onions. Core apples with a corer, then slice horizontally into ¼in/5mm rings. Trim ragged mushroom caps, peel off coarse skin. Slice onions into ¼in/5mm rings. Sprinkle all these foods with melted dripping or butter, if not smoke-cooking under sausages or bacon which will baste them. Place on the food carrier of a 'hot-box', or under it, and give a medium smoke.

Salt
Sprinkle on foil plates perforated with tiny holes, in a layer not more than ½in/1cm thick. Cold smoke for 3 – 4 hours, stirring from time to time to turn the salt over. It should be golden, and have a smoky aroma.

17
Processing Recipes and Ideas

White fish (eg cod, haddock)
Choose whole fish about 1lb/450g in weight, or larger fish yielding fillets of the same weight. Prepare as described in Chapter 16. Split whole fish (eg finnan haddie). Fillet larger fish, as described on page 120.

Soak in 70 – 80 per cent brine for about 15 minutes. Hang for 6 – 8 hours; since white fish has no flesh fat, it needs time to develop a glossy pellicle. Cold smoke at not more than 80°F/27°C until fish have lost about 12 – 13 per cent of their raw weight when prepared and are a very pale gold. Smaller fish weighing 8oz/225g should be brined for 6 – 8 minutes and lose only 8 – 10 per cent of weight.

Oily fish (eg mackerel, sardines, sprats)
Small fish under about 3oz/75g weight can be left whole or just have the guts squeezed out through a small slit. Remove fins of larger fish, gut and rinse. Leave heads on.

Soak mackerel in 70 – 80 per cent brine for up to 2 hours, depending on size; sardines and sprats will only need up to 10 minutes. Drain and rinse, since oily fish create their own gloss from the oil in their flesh. Lay very small fish on racks, or hang larger fish through the eyes, gills or throat, as in drawings 24 – 7, pages 121, 122; put wooden cocktail picks across the cavities of hanging fish to hold them open. Dry off for 30 minutes (sprats), 3 hours (mackerel).

Cold smoke at 80°F/27°C, giving mackerel up to 10 – 12 hours. The skins should be dry, mid-gold in colour; weight loss in larger fish should be about 25 per cent.

Hot smoke by increasing the heat to about 180°F/82.5°C after 4 – 6 hours cold-smoking time; maintain that heat for 2½ – 3 hours. Both skins and flesh will be darker in colour.

133

If you prefer, you can split mackerel or herring like haddock, pat dry with soft paper and smoke-cook; leave small fish whole, as above. Omit brining but salt and season flesh-sides of larger fish with herbs or pepper. Omit drying. (Sardines or sprats make excellent hot or cold cocktail snacks; behead after smoking, and serve with lemon wedges and thin slices of hot dry toast.)

Herring

Herring are processed in many ways, becoming, for instance, kippers or buckling. Kippers are herring that have been split and cold smoked (they can be eaten raw), while buckling are hot smoked whole, gutted from the neck end.

To make kippers, herring are scaled, then split through the belly, or through the length of the head and along the back close to the spine, leaving the belly skin intact. Clean and gut, remove the spine, then wash well. Although smaller, brine them like haddock, but only hang for an hour. Cold smoke until the fish are golden-brown and have lost about 12½ per cent of their prepared raw weight. It is impossible to give times, since herring vary so much in size and condition, apart from the usual variables such as the quantity of smoke, type of fuel and weather.

Buckling are a less common speciality dish with limited serving uses. A professional fish-smoker or manual should be consulted for these or similar speciality fish products.

Herring are less rewarding to smoke-cook than mackerel, tending to be harsh in flavour.

Salmon (and sea trout)

Salmon can be split like kippers or filleted (page 120). If you are not used to coping with large fish, practise your chosen technique on a smaller fish before handling a home-caught fish, or ask a fishmonger or fisherman to prepare one.

Wash off any blood carefully, and make sure you squeeze out any veins and remove any other marks on the flesh.

Brine lightly, especially frozen fish or any in poor condition. Most experts use a straight 80 per cent brine for newly-caught fish or a recipe similar to the one on page 90 for others. Leave for 1 – 5 hours, depending on the size and condition of the fish; salmon vary more than most fish, and you need an experienced eye. Do not over-salt; an under-brined product will still be tasty.

Hang for 18 – 24 hours, not less.

Start smoking at a lowish cold-smoking temperature, slightly under 80°F/27°C, for 7 – 9 hours until the flesh is lightly gilded. The fully smoked product should have lost 17 per cent of its prepared raw weight. Some experts continue smoking at around 80°F/27°C until the full loss is achieved; others raise the heat for an hour in three stages of 20 minutes each: first to 85°F/29.5°C, then to 90°F/32.5°C and finally to 100°F/37.8°C. This is of course much easier in an electrically powered smoker with a temperature gauge. (It is the method recommended by the makers of the Innes Walker smokers to develop the oil gloss.)

Salmon sides must be matured for at least 24 – 48 hours before being eaten.

Eels (conger and others)
Prepare the eels as described on page 120. Brine them in 80 per cent brine for 15 – 30 minutes (for conger). Dry off, hanging from hooks. Start smoking at normal cold-smoking temperature for about 2 hours, then increase the heat in stages, giving a slightly shorter time at each stage, and reaching a temperature of 170°F/76.5°C for a final ½ – 1 hour. Don't overcook. Weight loss should be 20 per cent from gutted raw weight.

Cod's roe
Brine in 70 per cent solution for 40 – 60 minutes in a thin muslin bag, and hang in the same bag to dry off. Cold smoke at 80°F/27°C for up to 24 hours until the covering membrane is a deep regal red.

Shellfish (prawns, mussels, oysters)
Smoke unpeeled or peeled *prawns* at 80°F/27°C for 1½ hours.

Smoke *mussels* in a preheated smoker at 160°F/71.5°C for 30 minutes, turning once.

Smoke *oysters* in the same way in a slightly hotter smoker, at 170°F/76.5°C for 30 minutes, turning if required to colour evenly.

Meat joints (beef, lamb, mutton)
Soak prepared meat joints in a flavoured brine or pickle, such as the General-use Sweet Brine on page 91, using the larger quantity of water. Leave for 2 days per lb/450g weight of meat in this pickle; when using others, vary the time accordingly, remembering that

lamb or mutton may need a slightly sweeter pickle than beef, and longer curing per lb/450g, especially if fatty.

Dry off for 12 – 24 hours. Then cold or hot smoke, or cold smoke and complete by roasting in an oven (lamb).

Smoking times as well as methods are very varied. Generally, lamb and especially mutton are coarser, fattier and stronger-flavoured than good-quality beef, so can take a sweeter cure, but need less seasoning; beef needs oiling after cold smoking, and benefits from rubbing with dry seasoning, whereas lamb and mutton do not need either. Cold smoke any meat at not more than 80°F/27°C, aiming at a total weight loss of 20 – 25 per cent from the prepared raw weight to the finished product, no matter what you will do to the meat after cold smoking it (if anything). While the finest-quality beef such as fillet can just be cold smoked, most fattier red-meat joints are probably best finished by hot smoking.

Generally, too, beef needs less smoking time than lamb or mutton. If beef has been well brined, and is to be hot smoked afterwards, 12 – 24 hours should be enough. Sweet-cured lamb or mutton joints may need 2 – 3 days. Keep a close eye on the process, because every joint varies in quality, depending on the animal's life-style and feed, whether the meat has been frozen or is fresh, and how well it was conditioned. Always be prepared to allow for variations which you do not know about and cannot assess by eye.

If you use the cold-smoking temperature and times above, insert a meat thermometer in beef, and hot smoke joints at 180°F/82°C for 2 hours, then raise the heat to 220°F/104°C until the thermometer registers an internal temperature of 140°F/60°C for rare beef, 158°F/70°C for medium-done beef, 167°F/75°C for well-done beef.

Also use a meat thermometer for lamb or mutton. Hot smoke at around 180°F/82°C for 2 hours, like beef, then raise the heat slightly less than for beef, and hot smoke to an internal temperature of 160°F/71°C to keep the juiciness of young lamb, 170°F/77°C for well-done older lamb or mutton.

If you want a mild smoked flavour, complete the cooking of any meat in the kitchen oven instead of hot smoking it, to the same internal temperatures. Alternatively, smoke-cook in a 'kettle' or tube-shaped portable smoker to the same internal temperatures, giving smoke for all or part of the time only.

Steaks, chops and burgers (any meat or meat mixture)
Steaks and chops are both best smoke-cooked. Rub or pound with
dry seasoning (page 127) if you wish. Oil well, then smoke. Eat
hot.

Burgers can be made wholly with fresh meat, or include some
pickled meat if not too salty. Oil lightly if lean, and smoke-cook.
Eat hot, or use like cold sausages for packed meals.

29 Smoked burger

Pork cuts and ham or bacon joints
There are more recipes, ancient and modern, for curing and
smoking pig-meat for ham and bacon than for any other meat, but
most are for whole hams or sides of bacon, unpractical for the
modern home craftsman. A 5lb/2.2kg boneless joint makes a good
mock old-style ham for a modern family; smaller, flatter pieces of
belly (bacon piece) or boned English spare rib about 2lb/1kg in
weight can be cured and smoked, then sliced like country-cured
bacon.

Mock ham can be dry-salted but is usually better brined or
pickled, using a sweet cure such as the Treacle and Ale Pickle on
page 92. Four 5lb/2.2kg pieces of boneless pork or cuts from the
fleshy part of the leg will probably take 10 days to cure in this
pickle. Drain and pat dry, then dry off well for at least 24 hours.
Cold smoke at 80°F/27°C for 24 hours or longer if you want a
sturdy smoked flavour. Dry well and hang in a cool, dark place
with plenty of air. Then wrap closely in cheesecloth, label and
store in a cold-room or cool larder with an even temperature, for
not more than 10 days. You would have to cure and smoke solid
meat cuts for longer than the times given to preserve them for

long-term storage. To use, boil, or take off the skin and bake, as you would a bought country-style ham.

Pickled and smoked pork belly (bacon piece) can be sliced and fried like bacon, and the same Treacle and Ale Pickle will give you a finely bronzed, delicious product. You can leave the pieces in the cure for up to 3 weeks if you want a really dark strong cure, but it will be too strong for breakfast bacon. A 2lb/1kg piece of averagely thick fatty meat should be ready in 4 – 6 days. Dry off well, then cold smoke like 'ham'. Again, use within 10 days.

For a less sweet 'mock bacon' cure, dry-salt pieces of the meat, using 1lb/450g mixed coarse and fine salt for 10lb/4.5kg meat. Rub in half the cure, keep at 38°F/3.5°C, and rub in the second half 3 days later. Cure for 2 days per lb/450g, turning the meat over occasionally. Brush off any cure on the surface of the meat, and dry off thoroughly. Cold smoke as above. Slice and fry like bacon.

As in all processing recipes, remember that the times suggested must be adapted if the condition of the meat or the weather requires it; eg if the meat is very thick and fatty, or the weather is warm or damp. Take particular care when processing pork to see that the pickle is always sweet-smelling and 'clean'. Aim at a weight loss of 22 – 24 per cent from the raw to the completed product.

Venison and strong game meats
Venison should hang for a week after slaughter before it is smoked, although it must not be 'high'. Being lean and inclined to be tough, it is probably best pickled. It should be hot smoked, and because of the animal's past life-style and the compact, sinewy texture of the meat, it must always be well 'cooked'.

Home-killed venison, especially, can vary immensely in age and condition as well as size and type. Besides this, various sizes and shapes of joints will probably have to be pickled and smoked at one time; it would be rare indeed to have six home-killed saddles of the same type and age to smoke at one time (although 'matching' joints can be bought to smoke for a large crowd on a special occasion). Pickling and smoking times will be as varied as the joints, and so provide for this by careful placement of the various pieces in the brine bath and smoker. If you are processing various different pieces at one time, attach a tag to each before brining, indicating how long it should stay in pickle.

You can use the Pickle for Furred Game on page 93, or adapt a favourite marinade of your own to give you an 80 per cent brine strength; most people who get home-killed venison regularly have one. Prick the meat well, all over, before pickling, and wipe off any blood. A tender saddle of venison will need 3 – 3½ hours in 80 per cent brine. Brine larger or thicker joints for proportionately longer; a whole haunch from the same beast would take at least twice as long in the brine, say 7 – 8 hours. Rinse the joints, and then dry off thoroughly for at least 24 hours in the case of thin pieces, such as a saddle. Keep cold or chilled while drying.

Cold smoke at around 70°F/21.5°C. Give a saddle 6 – 7 days. After 3 days, the meat will become blackish in colour.

Before hot smoking, massage the joint thoroughly with oil. Insert a meat thermometer in it. Hot smoke at 220°F/104°C for 2 – 3 hours, depending on the thickness. Take care not to overcook the dryer joints.

Sausages

To make your own sausages, you need a sausage-filling funnel, a filler supplied with a sausage-making 'kit', or an attachment on a large electric mixer. Sausage casings can be filled by hand but it is laborious work, and it is all too easy to fill the casings unevenly, making lumpy sausages with pockets of air between the lumps; they will then cook unevenly and tend to burst in the smoker.

You will also need casings; these may be natural (the intestines from a beef, mutton or pork carcass) or synthetic, made in similar sizes. For smoking, natural casings are best, although more nuisance to handle – they are stronger, taste better and take the smoke well – not all synthetic casings let the smoke penetrate them. Natural casings are also better-shaped, more elastic to allow for shrinkage, and easier to twist into links. Do not use very narrow casings for smoked sausages; the meat dries out too much.

Sausage casings are normally sold in very large quantities, far larger than any home craftsman is likely to need at a time; however, they freeze perfectly. If you do not want to store a large quantity, ask a kindly butcher to supply some processed casings – processing casings from a home-killed carcass is messy and not easy.

Different parts of an animal's intestines have different names; bungs are from the large intestine; middles and runners are smaller. The most usual casings for smoked sausages are ox (beef) and pig runners, and sheeps' middles. Natural casings are usually salted and must be soaked before use. Any not used should be re-salted before storing. Have the prepared, chopped or minced sausage-meat mixture in a convenient bowl. Open out the casing you will use by fitting the end over a cold tap and running the water through it. Measure it and cut off the length you want to use, say 6ft/1.8 metres; do not make it too long. Fit one end over the end of the funnel, the nozzle of a filler from a kit or the end of an attachment. Fill the funnel or the cylinder that feeds the nozzle or the appliance outlet, and push through enough mixture for one small sausage. Push it almost to the end of the casing, then tie the end of the casing in a knot or with string (if you knot it first there will be an air pocket between the knot and the first sausage-meat 'fill'). Continue filling the casing evenly and not too tightly, massaging with your hands to keep the quantity even; pinch the casing at equal intervals if you are making linked sausages. Knot or tie-off the top end of the sausage when the casing is full.

If you want to make your own sausage meat, a simple basic recipe is given below, and you can vary it as you like. The meat can be chopped or minced (generally chopped meat keeps moister). A cereal 'binder' can be added, or extra spices. Remember to use at least one-third fat to two-thirds meat in the mix, or the sausages may shrink too much and be tough and dry.

Basic pork sausage meat

1lb	450g	chilled lean, fresh, raw pork or lightly pickled pork, without skin or gristle	1lb
8oz	225g	chilled hard pork fat	8oz
2tsp	30ml	salt, or to taste (if using fresh pork)	2tsp
½tsp	2.5ml	ground white pepper	½tsp
½tsp	2.5ml	ground mace	½tsp
		pinch of ground ginger	
		pinch of powdered dried sage	

Chop the pork and fat together. Mix thoroughly and season to taste with the spices and herbs. Mince, using the coarse blade of the mincer. Mince again if you want a smoother sausage. Chill.

Stuff casings, and hang in a cool dark place for 24 hours to cure. Moisten to make casings elastic. Cold smoke at 80°F/26.5°C until dark chestnut in colour, or smoke-cook.

This quantity of mixture will make 12 sausages × 2oz/50g raw, but they will shrink a good deal in drying and smoking.

Treat the sausages like any other meat product which you salt and smoke. Brine most sausages in a straight 80 per cent brine; the mixture should already be well flavoured enough not to need pickling. The brining time will depend on the meat-mix and amount of fat. Most recipes for traditional cured and smoked sausages suggest not only a suitable brining time but also the traditional smoking method, fuel and time for that particular sausage. Home-made sausages can be cold or hot smoked. Take care when hot smoking, as the fat may 'turn' if kept at around 250°F/105°C for any length of time.

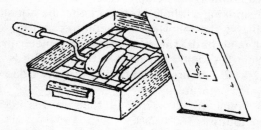

30 Assembled smoke cooker, with sausages

Sausages are, however, one of the most attractive and easy products to smoke-cook for quick use. Either home-made or cased commercial pork, beef or turkey sausages are all excellent, rich brown, sizzling and delicious. They can easily be given extra zip, too, as the recipes on pages 148 and 150 show.

Poultry, rabbit and game birds
Apart from duck, goose and water birds, all poultry and small game can be treated in much the same way. Having prepared the birds, and split or jointed them if you wish, the meat should first be brined in a fairly strong brine or pickle such as the General-use Sweet Brine on page 91, using the smaller quantity of water (60 per cent brine solution, approx). (For a turkey use the larger quantity of water and 2oz/50g more sugar.)

Pour the chilled brine over the bird or pieces in a tilted brine bath, and place a scalded board and weights on top. As examples

141

of curing times, leave a medium-sized whole prepared chicken or rabbit in the brine for 24 hours, a well-pricked 10lb/4.5kg turkey for 4 – 5 days, game birds for only an hour or so depending on size and type. Brine joints for proportionately less time.

Remove from the brine, rinse well with fresh water, and string for hanging as shown in drawing 21. Dry slowly and thoroughly or the flesh will harden. A chicken, for instance, may take 12 hours or more, a turkey at least 24 hours. Hang until no more drips fall from the cavity and the outside is dry.

Cold smoke at 70° – 80°F/21.4 – 26.5°C. As a guide to times, give a whole chicken 24 hours at the lower temperature, a whole turkey 5 – 7 days at the higher temperature. Guineafowl or pheasant will need about 18 hours at this temperature.

After cold smoking a whole bird can either be hot smoked or oven-roasted. Use the following temperatures and times for hot smoking. Oil game birds. Insert a meat thermometer in any bird before smoking. It should read 160°F/71°C for all birds.

Chicken: 2 – 2½ hours at 240°F/116°C (raised slowly from cold-smoking temperature).

Turkey: 8 hours at 170°F/76.5°C, then at 185°F/85°C until internal temperature is 160°F/71°C.

Guineafowl: 1 hour at 240°F/116°C (raised like chicken).

Pheasant: 15 minutes at 210°F/99°C, then test frequently or until meat thermometer reads 160°F/71°C.

Rabbit: 1 hour at 180°F/82°C or until tender.

The final weight loss should be about 20 per cent.

All birds can be 'kettle'-smoked for all or part of their cooking time.

Joints will, of course, take a much shorter time than those above, which are for whole birds.

Instead of cold and hot smoking, all joints are excellent smoke-cooked in a 'hot-box'. Oil well, sprinkle with chopped dried herbs or spices if you wish (not salt), and give medium to strong smoking.

Duck

A special case because of its fat content. A 4lb/2kg duck (dressed weight) must be pricked thoroughly and deeply, and can then be immersed in 80 per cent plain or spiced brine or pickle. Brine this size of duck for about 2½ hours. String, and hang up to dry for 24

142

hours. Cold smoke, if possible in very cool smoke, at 60°F/15.5°C and at not more than 70°F/21.5°C for about 2 days at the lower temperature, or 36 hours at the higher one. Then hot smoke at 180°F/82°C for 3 hours, raise the temperature to 240°F/116°C and smoke for about 2 hours longer or until a meat thermometer reads 185°F/85°C.

Other products
Processing these is covered on pages 131–2.

'HOT-BOX' AND 'KETTLE'-SMOKED FOODS

The general method of 'hot' or smoke-box cooking described on pages 105–106 can be applied to all small pieces of food of any type, the only differences being in the flavouring. Since the alternatives are largely a matter of choice, there is no need to give special recipes for them.

Like 'hot-box' smoke-cooking, 'kettle'-smoking can be used for brined, semi-brined or marinated, or unbrined foods; however, the food can be partly cooked without smoke at the beginning of its cooking time if you wish. It will not affect the actual cooking time of the food, but its appearance will be different, and it is therefore wise always to use a meat thermometer as a guide to when meats, poultry or game are fully cooked.

Apart from your choice to add the smoking fuel when you wish, they are all processed in the same way.

Soak the smoking fuel you will use (wood chips of various sizes) in clean water.

Open all the bottom vents on the 'kettle'. Build a small charcoal fire in the bottom of the kettle's bowl or in some models on the charcoal grid. When the fire is going well, put racks in place loaded with the food, open top and close bottom vents and start cooking. Top up the charcoal when necessary for long-cooking items such as turkey. When it suits you, or a recipe in the manufacturer's instruction manual recommends it, add the smoking fuel to the fire. Cook until the meat thermometer registers that flesh foods are done. In using recipes for fish or 'made-up' dishes, follow the manufacturer's instructions.

Here is a sample recipe:

Smoked loin of pork

5 – 6lb	2.5 – 3kg	boned, rolled loin of pork	5 – 6lb
1	1	garlic clove, slivered	1
½tsp	2.5ml	each of celery salt, dried crushed rosemary, dried basil	½tsp
¼tsp	1.25ml	white pepper	¼tsp
1 tsp	5ml	caraway seeds	1 tsp

Soak hardwood chips and get a charcoal fire well alight in the kettle. Make small slits in the top of the boned and rolled joint, and insert a sliver of garlic in each slit. Mix all the spices and sprinkle over the meat. Add the smoking fuel to the fire. Place the roast on the cooking grill, close the kettle lid and bottom vents, and smoke-cook for 6 hours or until a meat thermometer registers 170°F/76.5°C. Top up the fuels when necessary during cooking (see drawing 16).

(For information in this chapter, the author is indebted to Kate and Frank Walker.)

18
Recipes Using Smoked Foods

STARTERS

Smoked eel with horseradish butter
For each person, arrange small thin strips of skinned smoked eel in a star pattern on a small plate with a sprig of watercress in the centre. Hand round hot, freshly made dry toast and pats of chilled horseradish butter, with lemon wedges for squeezing.

Smoked sprats, whole but beheaded, can be served in the same way. Allow 6 – 8 sprats per person, depending on size.

Horseradish Butter

6 oz	175g	softened butter	¾ cup
3tbsp	45ml	freshly grated horseradish	3tbsp
		a few drops of lemon juice	

Whip the butter until light. Rinse and dry the horseradish, and work it into the butter with a little lemon juice. Chill at once, and use within 48 hours. (This quantity of butter serves 4 people.)

Taramasalata *Serves 6*

4oz	100g	smoked cod's roe, skinned	¼lb
½pt	275ml	olive oil	1¼ cups
1tbsp	15ml	finely chopped (minced) onion	1tbsp
		juice of ½ lemon	
1tsp	5ml	chopped fresh parsley	1tsp
2tbsp	30ml	fresh white breadcrumbs	2tbsp
		freshly ground black pepper to taste	

Break up the roe with a fork in a bowl. Add half the oil, and let stand for 30 minutes. Blend until smooth in a food processor or blender, while adding the remaining oil and the lemon juice. Return to the bowl, and stir in the remaining ingredients.

Serve with pitta bread, lightly toasted.

Smoked cod's roe pâté or dip *Serves 4*

4oz	100g	smoked cod's roe, skinned	4oz
4oz	100g	full fat soft cheese (unflavoured)	½ cup
1	1	small onion, grated	1
		juice of ½ lemon	

Soak the roe for 5 minutes in hot water to get rid of some of the salt. Drain on soft kitchen paper. Put the roe in a bowl with the cheese and onion, and work with the back of a spoon until fully blended and creamy, adding the lemon juice gradually while doing so. Serve slightly chilled in small pots or a single bowl, with hot dry toast.

Smoked salmon rolls *Serves 4*

4	4	large slices thin-cut smoked salmon	4
1 tbsp	15ml	butter	1tbsp
8	8	eggs	8
		salt and ground white pepper to taste	
6tbsp	90ml	soured cream	6tbsp
2tsp	10ml	finely chopped (minced) parsley	2tsp

Trim any ragged edges on the salmon slices and lay flat. Whisk the eggs in a bowl with a few grains of salt and a sprinkling of pepper. Melt the butter in a frying-pan over low heat, pour in the eggs, and scramble lightly until set. Spread ¼ of the scrambled egg over each smoked salmon slice. Roll up the slices like Swiss rolls. Place in a shallow dish. Spoon the soured cream over the rolls, and sprinkle with chopped parsley.

Artichokes protea *Serves 4*

4	4	large French globe artichokes	4
		salt	
½pt	275ml	well-flavoured white sauce, cooled	1¼ cups
2	2	egg yolks	2
2tbsp	30ml	single cream	2tbsp
		smoked-salmon trimmings, shredded	
2tsp	10ml	lemon juice	2tsp
		cayenne pepper	

Twist off the artichoke stems (do not cut them off). Trim the tops of the leaves square except for those of the centre cone. Stand the artichokes upright in a pan of slightly salted boiling water, cover the pan, and boil them gently until the leaves move easily, 35 – 45 minutes for large artichokes. Turn upside-down to drain. Cool until tepid.

While boiling the artichokes, start making the sauce. Skim any skin off the white sauce. Mix together the egg yolks and cream. Stir in a little of the sauce, then return the mixture to the rest of the sauce.

Remove the centre cone of small leaves from the artichokes, exposing the furry choke. Remove it by scraping it out with a teaspoon, to expose the base. Fill the artichoke cups with the shredded smoked salmon; the quantity needed depends on the size of the artichokes. Place one pink-centred artichoke 'flower' in each of 4 small bowls.

Just before serving, warm the sauce gently to cook the egg yolks; do not let it boil. Flavour it with the lemon juice, a little salt and cayenne pepper. Serve in a warmed jug with the 'proteas'.

Smoked trout with soured-cream dressing *Serves 4*

2	2	whole hot-smoked or smoke-cooked trout	2
6oz	175g	full fat soft cheese (unflavoured)	¾ cup
1	1	hard-boiled (hard-cooked) egg	1
1tsp	5ml	capers	1tsp
1tsp	5ml	vinegar from caper jar	1tsp
		pinch of salt	
5tbsp	75ml	soured cream	5tbsp
		watercress sprigs	

Skin and fillet the trout, and arrange one fillet, skinned side up, on each of 4 plates. Soften the cheese if required. Pipe it in lines around the edge of each fillet and in a decorative line along its centre. Chill. Chop the egg finely, or mince it, with the capers. Mix together the vinegar, salt and cream. Fold in the egg mixture. Chill in a jug.

To serve, garnish the fillets with watercress sprigs. Serve the sauce separately.

Note: If you wish, use 2 eggs and 2 tsp/10ml capers. Add half the mixture to the dressing, then sprinkle the rest over and around the garnished fillets.

Chicken and melon starter *Serves 4*

1	1	small honeydew melon	1
4oz	100g	smoked chicken meat without bone	4oz
4	4	large leaves of fresh mint	4
4fl oz	100ml	soured cream	½ cup
		salt and ground black pepper	

Quarter the melon lengthways, and cut the flesh into small cubes. Season with a little salt and pepper. Put the cubes into 4 small bowls or dessert glasses. Chop the chicken meat into small pieces with the mint leaves. Mix with the melon cubes. Shortly before serving, top with the soured cream and season with a little more pepper.

Namaqualand beef *Serves 4*

2tbsp	30ml	corn oil	2tbsp
2tbsp	30ml	white wine vinegar	2tbsp
		salt and pepper	
¼tsp	1.25ml	French mustard	¼tsp
		pinch of sugar (optional)	
2	2	large firm ripe avocado pears	2
4oz	100g	smoked beef cut in small thin strips	¼lb

Make a French dressing with the oil, vinegar, seasonings and sugar. Halve the avocado pears lengthways, remove the stones, and sprinkle all over with dressing. Pile the smoked-beef shreds into the hollows left by the stones. Sprinkle with dressing, and serve with fingers of hot dry thin toast.

FINGER FOOD

Smoked sausage cocktail pasties *Makes 24 – 28 snacks*

8oz	225g	plain flour	2 cups
½tsp	2.5ml	salt	½tsp
2oz	50g	hard block margarine (at room temperature)	¼ cup
1tsp	5ml	bicarbonate of soda	1tsp
2tsp	10ml	cream of tartar	2tsp
4fl oz	100ml	milk	½ cup
2	2	long frankfurter-style smoked sausages, 1½ oz/35g each	2
1½oz	35g	Cheddar cheese	1½oz
		mild mustard	

Sift the flour and salt into a bowl. Rub in the fat until the 'mix' is like breadcrumbs. Mix in the raising agents. Bind with enough milk to make a dough which leaves the bowl cleanly.

On a lightly floured surface, knead the dough for about ½ minute. Roll it out thinly and cut it into 2in/5cm rounds. Re-roll trimmings and cut out. Cut the sausages into slices about ¼in/6mm thick, discarding the ends; they should cover half the rounds. Place one slice in the centre of each round, and top each with a sliver of cheese and dab of mustard. Damp the edges of the covered dough rounds and cover with the remaining rounds. Press the edges to seal. Make a small slit in the top of each pasty and brush with milk. Bake at 400°F/200°C/Gas 6 for 10 – 12 minutes. Serve hot or warm.

Note: Mashed smoked fish can be used instead of sausage.

Smoked cheeseburgers *Serves 6*

1	1	15oz/425g can butter beans, drained (navy beans)	1
		pinch of grated nutmeg	
		a few drops lemon juice	
½tsp	2.5ml	salt	½tsp
¼tsp	1.25ml	pepper	¼tsp
½	½	medium onion, finely chopped	½
1	1	egg, beaten	1
1tsp	5ml	tomato ketchup	1tsp
3oz	75g	flour	¼ cup
2oz	50g	chopped mixed nuts	¼ cup
6	6	square slices smoked cheese, about 3in/75mm	6
1tbsp	15ml	softened butter	1tbsp
		apricot chutney	
6	6	soft round rolls	6

Process the beans and seasonings to a paste in a food processor or blender. Mix in the onion, then the egg and ketchup. Add the flour and nuts by hand. Shape into a ball and chill for about 30 minutes.

Form the bean paste into 12 flat circles a little smaller than the rolls. Trim the cheese squares into circles a little smaller still. Keep the cheese trimmings. Place one cheese circle on each of 6 bean-paste 'pancakes' and cover it with another. Press to enclose the cheese. Place the 'burgers' on a well-greased and floured baking sheet. Brush with softened butter. Shred the cheese trimmings and put a pinch on each 'burger'. Bake at 350°F/180°C/

149

Gas 4 for 20 minutes. Top with a dab of chutney and place in split and buttered hot rolls.

Use for an informal snack meal or on any occasion such as a Guy Fawkes party.

Smoked beef or ham snacks *Makes 24 cocktail snacks*

3oz	75g	full-fat soft cheese (unflavoured)	3oz
1tbsp	15ml	horseradish cream from jar	1tbsp
5 – 6 slices	5 – 6 slices	thinly cut smoked beef or Parma ham	5 – 6 slices

Mix together the cheese and horseradish. Spread the mixture on the meat. Roll up the meat slices like baby Swiss rolls and chill until firm. Slice across with a sharp knife. Serve on small round cocktail biscuits.

Banger splits (sausages with cheese) *Makes 8 snacks*
(Hot-box smoke-cooking)

8	8	small beef sausages 1oz/25g each	8
1½oz	35g	Edam cheese in one thick piece	1½oz
8	8	small wholemeal finger rolls	8
		chutney (sweet pickle) to taste	
		butter for spreading	

Split the sausages lengthways, leaving one long side joined. Cut the cheese into 8 sticks, just shorter than the sausages. Spread the inside of each sausage with a little chutney (sweet pickle) and insert 1 cheese stick. Press to close. Put the sausages on the food carrier of a 'hot-box' smoke-cooker, and give them light or medium strong smoke processing.

Meanwhile, split the rolls in the same way as the sausages. Butter the cut sides, put on an aluminium-foil plate, and cover with foil. Place on top of the smoke-box to warm. When the sausages are smoked, put 1 sausage into each roll. Serve at once.

Good for a brunch or a barbecue party.

MAIN DISHES

Smoked mackerel and corn chowder *Serves 6*

1¼lb	560g	sweet corn kernels, canned or frozen	1¼lb
8oz	225g	potatoes	½lb
		salt and pepper	
1	1	onion, coarsely chopped	1
2	2	celery stalks, thinly sliced	2
3tbsp	45ml	butter or margarine	3tbsp
4 – 5oz	100 – 150g	hot-smoked or smoke-cooked mackerel fillet, skinned and flaked	4 – 5oz
¾oz	20g	flour	¾oz
¾ – 1pt	425 – 550ml	milk	2 – 2½ cups
1½oz	40g	butter	1½oz

Drain, or thaw and drain, the corn. Keep aside. Peel the potatoes and cut into ¾in/2cm dice. In a large saucepan, boil the potato dice in ¾pt/425ml (2 cups) water for 5 minutes; reduce the heat, cover the pan, and simmer for another 5 – 10 minutes until the dice are tender. Draw off the heat.

Fry the onion and celery in a saucepan in 2tbsp/30ml of the fat until the onion is gilded. Remove with a slotted spoon, and add to the potatoes with the flaked mackerel. Add the remaining 1tbsp/15ml fat to the pan used for frying. Sprinkle in the flour and stir for 2 minutes over low heat. Gradually add the milk, stirring constantly, and bring to the boil. Pour over the potato mixture, then stir in the corn and butter. Reheat gently for 5 – 10 minutes until bubbling. Serve hot in large soup-bowls as a supper dish.

Omelet John Buchan *Serves 2*

4oz	100g	cooked finnan haddock boned	4oz
2oz	50g	butter	¼ cup
¼ pt	150ml	double (heavy) cream	½ cup + 2 tbsp
3	3	eggs, separated	3
2tbsp	30ml	grated Parmesan cheese	2tbsp
		salt	
		freshly ground black pepper	

Flake the fish, place in a saucepan and add 2tbsp/30ml butter and 2tbsp/30ml cream. Toss until the butter melts, then remove the pan from the heat. Beat the egg-yolks with 1tbsp/15ml more cream and 1tbsp/15ml cheese. Stir in the fish mixture. Whisk the egg-whites stiffly and fold them in. Melt the remaining butter in an omelet pan. Make the omelet as usual, but do not fold it. Instead, cover it with remaining cheese and cream, and slide under the grill until bubbling. Serve at once, with green peas.

Sunrise smoked herring *Serves 4*

2tbsp	30ml	butter	2tbsp
4	4	carrots, finely chopped	4
2	2	medium onions, chopped	2
1	1	garlic clove, chopped	1
2tbsp	30ml	chopped parsley	2tbsp
1	1	bay leaf	1
¼tsp	1.5ml	dried thyme	¼tsp
		good grinding of black pepper	
		good pinch of ground allspice	
8oz	225g	smoked herring (any style), boned and filleted	8oz
		lemon juice	
2tbsp	30ml	chilled cottage cheese	2tbsp

Melt the butter in a large, deep frying pan or skillet. Add the carrot, onion, garlic, parsley and bay leaf and pour in just enough water to cover them. Sprinkle with the thyme, pepper and allspice. Lay the herring fillets on top. Cover with a lid or spatter-proof cover. Bring gently to simmering point, and cook for 12 – 15 minutes until the vegetables are tender. Remove the herring fillets with a perforated slice to a warmed plate. Drain the vegetables thoroughly and place in a shallow, warmed serving dish. Skin the herring fillets and arrange on the dish. Sprinkle the dish with lemon juice, and top each fillet with soft cheese. Serve hot.

Cottage cheese gives more of a pleasant tang to this dish than a full-fat soft cheese, and lets the flavour of the butter and herbs 'come through'.

Baked avocados and smoked fish *Serves 4*

2	2	avocado pears	2
		lemon juice	
6 – 8oz	175 – 225g	smoked cod or haddock without skin and bones	6 – 8oz
		salt if needed	
		pepper	
		browned breadcrumbs (optional)	
		butter	

Halve the avocados lengthways and remove the stones. Take out most of the flesh in curls or shreds with a teaspoon, leaving 4 firm shells. Toss the shredded flesh in a bowl with enough lemon juice to prevent it discolouring. Flake the fish and mix it with the avocado shreds. Season to taste. Pile the mixture back in the avocado-skin shells. Cover with crumbs if you wish. Dot generously with butter. Place cut-side-up on a greased baking sheet. Cover loosely with greased foil, and bake at 350°F/180°C/Gas 4 for 20 minutes.

Serve hot as a first course; or double the quantities for a light lunch and serve with sliced green beans.

For a quick starter, serve the stuffed avocado shells cold, without crumbs, topped with a dab of thick yoghurt or soft smooth curd cheese.

Smoked fish croquettes *Serves 4 – 6* (12 croquettes)

1lb	450g	any smoked fish, skinned, boned and flaked	1lb
3oz	75g	soft white breadcrumbs	3oz
½tsp	2.5ml	French mustard	½tsp
4tsp	20ml	lemon juice	4tsp
2 – 4tbsp	30 – 60ml	cold bread sauce (from pkt)	2 – 4tbsp
2	2	eggs, beaten	2
		Melba toast crumbs for coating	
		oil for shallow frying	
1	1	small carton coleslaw (optional)	1

Mix together the fish and breadcrumbs in a bowl. Stir the mustard into the lemon juice, and use to moisten the fish mixture. Mash the mixture until fairly smooth (ideally done in a food processor). Mix in enough bread sauce to make a mixture which can be moulded. (The quantity will depend on the type of fish, and on how moist it is.) Form into cork or sausage shapes, about the same size and shape as large pork sausages. Brush well with beaten egg, then roll in crumbs to coat thoroughly. Leave to stand for 30 minutes. Fry in shallow oil, turning as required until crisp and golden all over.

Serve on shredded lettuce as a dinner-party first course, or for brunch or a midnight party 'breakfast', garnished with coleslaw, and with lemon wedges.

153

Kipper soufflé (kippered herring soufflé) *Serves 4*

1lb	450g	boned kipper (kippered herring) or kipper fillets	1lb
2tbsp	30ml	cornflour (cornstarch)	2tbsp
½pt	275ml	milk	1¼ cups
1tbsp	15ml	butter	1tbsp
2oz	50g	Cheddar cheese, grated	¼ cup
2	2	eggs, separated	2
		salt and pepper	

Grease a 2pt/1.1 litre soufflé dish. Cook, skin and flake the fish. Blend the cornflour (cornstarch) with 2tbsp/30ml of the milk. Bring the rest of the milk to the boil, with the butter, pour onto the cornflour while stirring, then return the mixture to the pan. Heat until it boils, stirring all the time. As soon as the sauce thickens, stir in the cheese and egg yolks briskly; then fold in the fish, taste and season if required. Whisk the egg whites stiffly and fold into the soufflé mixture. Turn into the prepared dish, and bake at 400°F/200°C/Gas 6 for 20 minutes.

Serve immediately with fingers of puff pastry and a garnish of cucumber salad.

Creamy smoked cod *Serves 4*

1lb	450g	smoked cod fillet	1lb
½pt	275ml	milk	1¼ cups
1½oz	35g	butter	7tsp
4tbsp	60ml	flour	4tbsp
4oz	100g	grated Cotswold cheese	½ cup
		salt, pepper	
		chopped chives	

Cover the fish with cold water, and bring slowly to the boil. Put a lid on the pan, turn off the heat, and leave for 15 minutes. Strain off ¼pt/150ml/½ cup + 2tbsp of the cooking liquid into a jug and add the milk to it. Discard the remaining cooking liquid. Skin, bone and flake the fish. In a fairly large, clean pan, melt the butter, stir in the flour, and stir for 2 minutes without colouring. Stir in the cooking liquid and milk gradually, bring to the boil and stir until thickening. Stir in the cheese and a little seasoning, then fold in the fish. Serve in scallop shells, sprinkling each helping with chopped chives.

Florence Nightingale's kedgeree *Serves 4 – 5*

6oz	175g	long-grain rice	6oz
		salt	
12oz	335g	smoked haddock fillet	¾lb
1	1	onion, chopped	1
4oz	100g	butter	½ cup
3	3	hard-boiled (hard-cooked) eggs	3
1tbsp	15ml	grated Parmesan cheese	1tbsp
		fried bread triangles	

Tip the rice into boiling salted water, and boil fast for 11 – 12 minutes. Drain. While cooking, pour boiling water over the fish; leave to stand for 5 minutes. Meanwhile, simmer the onion in a large pan, using a little of the butter until gilded. Skin and flake the fish and mix in the onion, leaving the fat in the pan. Chop the hard-boiled egg whites and mix with the fish. Sieve the yolks onto a plate and mix in the cheese.

Add the remaining butter to that left from frying the onion, melt it and toss the rice in it over gentle heat until well coated and hot. Mix in the fish, onion and egg-white mixture. Pile on an ovenproof platter. Sprinkle the egg yolk and cheese on top. Place in the oven at 350°F/180°C/Gas 4 until the cheese begins to colour.

Serve surrounded with the fried bread triangles.

'Kettle'-smoked whole fish

8 – 10lb	3.6 – 4.5kg	large whole fish	8 – 10lb
4fl oz	100ml	lemon juice	½ cup
1tbsp	15ml	Worcestershire sauce	1tbsp
1tbsp	15ml	made mustard	1tbsp
½tsp	2.5ml	dried basil	½tsp
½tsp	2.5ml	garlic salt	½tsp
½tsp	2.5ml	table salt	½tsp
1	1	medium onion, thinly sliced	1
1	1	lemon, thinly sliced	1
		melted butter or oil	

Clean and prepare the fish. Mix together the lemon juice, Worcestershire sauce, mustard, basil and both salts. Brush over the cavity of the fish. Arrange half the onion and lemon slices alternately in a row, in the cavity of the fish. Brush the outside of the fish with fat or oil. Arrange the remaining onion and lemon slices in a row on top of the fish.

Oil the cooking grill of the 'kettle', and place a bowl of water on the grill (or fill the pan provided). Place the fish on the grill. Sprinkle with remaining lemon mixture. Cover and smoke-cook for 3 – 4 hours until done. Carve small portions on the grill.

Cannelloni with smoked beef *Serves 4*

8	8	cannelloni tubes	8
1tbsp	15ml	olive oil	1tbsp
12oz	335g	frozen chopped spinach, thawed and drained	12oz
6oz	175g	mozzarella cheese, shredded	6oz
4oz	100g	smoked beef, cut in small thin strips	4oz
¾pt	425g	white sauce	2 cups
		pinch of grated nutmeg	
1oz	25g	dry white breadcrumbs	1oz
1oz	25g	Parmesan cheese	1oz
6pt	3.4litres	boiling water	7½pt
		salt and pepper	

Boil the cannelloni in the water with salt to taste and the oil for about 15 minutes. Drain, dip in cold water, than drain again. Lay the tubes side by side on a damp cloth.

Chop the spinach finely, and mix in the cheese. Season lightly with salt and pepper. Put the spinach mixture into the cannelloni tubes and lay them side by side in a greased, shallow oven-to-table baking dish. Spread any leftover stuffing over them. Scatter the strips of beef on top. Season the white sauce with a very little salt, a good grinding of pepper and the nutmeg. Pour it over the beef.

Bake at 350°F/180°C/Gas Mark 4 for 20 minutes. Mix together the breadcrumbs and Parmesan, and sprinkle over the dish. Place under medium grill heat to brown the surface of the dish.

Kidney 'olives' *Serves 4*
(Hot-box smoke-cooking)

4	4	lamb kidneys	4
		salt, ground black pepper	
2tsp	10ml	dried crushed thyme	2tsp
1	1	medium onion, thinly sliced	1
2 – 3	2 – 3	bay leaves	2 – 3
4fl oz	100ml	medium sherry	½ cup
2tbsp	30ml	corn oil	2tbsp
8	8	rashers (slices) rindless bacon	8
8oz	225g	mashed potato	1 cup

Split the kidneys, skin and core them. Sprinkle them with salt, pepper and thyme. Lay them in a bowl with the onion. Put the bay leaves on top, and pour the sherry and oil over them. Leave in a cool place for 4 hours. Turn the kidneys over after 2 hours' soaking.

Drain the kidneys. Wrap a bacon rasher (slice) round each one. Secure with wooden cocktail picks. Place the kidneys on the food carrier of a hot-box smoke-cooker. Give them medium-smoke processing.

Meanwhile, reheat the mashed potato if required. Place it on a warmed serving dish. Keep warm. When smoking is completed, lay the 'olives' on the potato.

Serve at once, with French mustard and tomato ketchup, or with sweet pickle.

Lamb kebabs *Serves 4*
(Hot-box smoke-cooking)

8oz	225g	lean lamb from leg or shoulder	½lb
		salt and ground black pepper	
2tbsp	30ml	tomato paste from can or tube	2tbsp
1tbsp	15ml	French mustard	1tbsp
20	20	small button mushrooms	20
		cooking oil for brushing	
8oz	225g	egg noodles	½lb
1	1	medium onion	1
		butter	

Cut the meat into 1 in/2.5cm cubes. Season with salt and pepper. Mix together the tomato paste and mustard. Coat the meat cubes with the mixture and put aside for 1 hour. Thread the cubes on 4 skewers, alternating them with mushrooms. Brush with oil.

Give the kebabs medium smoking in a hot-box smoke-cooker. Meanwhile, boil the noodles as directed on the packet. Skin and slice the onion, and fry in butter until soft and lightly browned. Drain the noodles when ready, mix with the onion and any remaining frying butter, and pile on a warmed serving dish. Keep warm. When the kebabs are smoked, lay them on the pasta and serve at once.

Note: You could use lean beef instead of lamb.

German boiled bacon *Serves 4*

1	1	15oz/425g can haricot beans	1
8oz	225g	frozen sliced green beans, thawed	8oz
2tsp	10ml	grated cheese	2tsp
		salt and pepper	
2	2	firm eating pears	2
2	2	sharp apples	2
8oz	225g	rindless smoked back bacon rashers (slices)	8oz

Turn the beans and the liquid in the can into a 2½pt/1.4 litre casserole. Cover with the sliced green beans. Sprinkle with the cheese and season well. Core and slice the pears and layer on the beans. Cut the smoked rashers in half across and place half of them in an overlapping layer on the pears. Quarter, core and segment the apples and arrange on top. Cover with the remaining bacon rashers. Put a lid on the casserole, place over medium heat and bring to the boil. Reduce the heat and simmer for 40 minutes.

Papet vaudois *Serves 4*

2¼lb	1kg	leeks	2¼lb
3	3	large potatoes	3
		bacon fat	
		chicken stock as needed	
1tbsp	15ml	flour	1tbsp
2tsp	10ml	milk	2tsp
		salt and pepper	
		pinch each dried thyme, basil and grated nutmeg	
4	4	thick smoked bacon or ham slices (cooked)	4
4	4	hot-smoked pork slices about 2½in/6cm diameter, or hot-smoked pork cutlets	4

Prepare and slice leeks, and peel and slice potatoes. Melt a knob of bacon fat in a heavy pan, add the vegetables and cover with stock. Simmer over low heat until the potato slices are tender, depending on type and thickness. With a slotted spoon, remove the vegetables to a shallow ovenproof dish greased with bacon fat. Arrange the bacon or ham slices in an overlapping line on the vegetables, with the pork slices or cutlets on top. Blend the flour with the milk, and stir into the vegetable cooking liquid. Pour over the dish. Bake at 350°F/180°C/Gas 4 loosely covered with greased foil for 20 – 25 minutes until the meats are well heated through.

Bake-fried turkey in almonds *Serves 4*

4	4	serving portions of hot-smoked or smoke-cooked turkey, eg halved breast fillets	4
1oz	25g	flour	¼ cup
		salt and pepper	
½tsp	2.5ml	paprika	½tsp
1	1	large egg	1
1	1	egg yolk	1
4oz	100g	flaked almonds, crushed	4oz
4 – 5tbsp	60 – 75ml	butter, margarine or chicken fat	4 – 5tbsp

Heat the oven to 375°F/190°C/Gas 5. Skin the turkey meat if required. Mix the flour and seasonings, and coat the turkey portions with seasoned flour. Beat the egg and the extra yolk together. Scatter the crushed almond flakes on stout paper. Brush the turkey portions with egg all over, then coat with crushed almonds, pressing the flakes on firmly. Leave to stand for 20 minutes. Meanwhile, heat the fat in the preheated oven in a shallow baking tin (pan) which will hold the portions side by side.

Place the portions in the hot tin, fleshy side down if they contain bone. Bake for 20 minutes. Turn the portions over and bake for another 10 – 15 minutes until golden. Drain and lay on a heated platter.

Serve with finely sliced green beans and potato straws.

Cretan smoked chicken bake *Serves 4*

1	1	medium aubergine	1
4tbsp	60ml	olive or sunflower oil	4tbsp
1	1	medium onion, chopped	1
3	3	medium tomatoes, skinned and chopped	3
4oz	100g	cooked green peas	4oz
½tsp	2.5ml	dried oregano leaves	½tsp
1tbsp	15ml	fresh chopped parsley	1tbsp
¼tsp	1.5ml	salt	¼tsp
		freshly ground black pepper	
6oz	175g	smoked chicken meat cut in small thin slices	6oz
4fl oz	100ml	chicken stock (from cube)	½ cup
		butter for dotting	

Cut off the aubergine stem, and slice the fruit thinly lengthways. In a large frying pan, sauté the slices in batches using 3tbsp/45ml of the oil; cook until browned on both sides, then transfer to soft paper until all the slices are fried. Add the remaining 1tbsp/15ml

159

oil while frying if needed. Draw the pan to the side of the stove when all the slices are fried. Use half the slices to line the base of a shallow oven-to-table baking dish.

Add the onion to the oil in the pan, return it to the heat, and sauté the onion until soft and golden. Add the tomatoes, peas, oregano, parsley and seasoning. Mix well with the onion, then turn the contents of the pan into the baking dish and spread the mixture over the aubergine. Arrange the chicken meat slices in a neat layer on top. Pour the stock into the dish, and dot the surface with butter. Cover loosely with foil and bake for 15 – 20 minutes at 350°F/180°C/Gas 4. Serve hot.

Smoked poultry or game-meat pie *Serves 4 – 6*

2	2	large leeks, sliced (white parts only)	2
½	½	medium onion, thinly sliced	½
12 – 14oz	335 – 400g	smoked poultry or game-bird meat, or a mixture, without skin	12 – 14 oz
2	2	large (2oz/50g) smoked sausages	2
2	2	hard-boiled (hard-cooked) eggs	2
		sprinkling of dried mixed herbs	
		sprinkling of grated nutmeg	
		salt and ground black pepper	
		well-flavoured chicken stock as needed	
6oz	175g	puff pastry	6oz
		beaten egg for glazing	

Cook the sliced leeks and onion in boiling salted water until just tender. Drain. Chop the poultry or game-bird meat into small pieces, and slice the sausages. Mix together. Pack half the meat mixture into a 1¼pt/700ml (3¼ cup) deep pie-dish. Sprinkle with herbs, nutmeg and seasoning. Slice the hard-boiled eggs and lay on top, then the vegetables in an even layer. Pack the remaining meat on top, and sprinkle with a little more herbs, nutmeg and seasoning. Pour in enough stock to half-fill the dish.

Roll out the pastry, and use it to cover and decorate the dish. Make a small escape hole for steam in the centre. Bake at 400°F/200°C/Gas 6 for 30 minutes. Glaze with beaten egg, and return to the oven for 7 – 8 minutes to set the glaze. Serve hot.

Note: If you wish to serve the pie cold, use jellied stock, melted. When the pie is cooked, fill it up with extra stock through the steam escape hole.

Smoked duck risotto *Serves 6*

12oz	335g	brown rice	2 cups
1	1	small onion, chopped	1
3oz	75g	chicken fat or butter	⅓ cup
1tsp	5ml	tomato paste	1tsp
1oz	25g	shelled peas	1oz
2tbsp	30ml	seedless raisins	2tbsp
		good pinch of dried mixed herbs	
		salt and pepper	
1¾pt	1litre	stock or water from cooking vegetables	4½ cups
2tsp	10ml	dry white vermouth	2tsp
8 – 9oz	225 – 250g	smoked duck meat, skinned and cut in small strips	8 – 9oz
1oz	25g	button mushrooms, sliced	1oz

Wash the rice. Add the onion to half the fat in a large heavy saucepan, and fry gently until soft. Add the rice and tomato paste, and stir well for 2 – 3 minutes. Add the peas, raisins and herbs. Season well. In another pan, heat the stock or water and vermouth to scalding; draw off the heat. Add ¼pt/150ml (½ cup + 2tbsp) of the hot liquid to the rice and vegetables. Simmer until it is absorbed. Repeat this process twice more. Then add the rest of the liquid, half-cover the pan and reduce the heat to a low simmer. Cook for about 20 minutes, stirring occasionally. Add the diced duck meat and mushrooms, and continue simmering until the rice is tender, the liquid is absorbed and the duck is well heated (another 15 – 20 minutes as a rule). Add a little hot water if the rice looks like drying out. Reseason before serving if needed.

Serve very hot with chutney and salad.

Smoked cheese and mushroom soufflé *Serves 4*

3oz	75g	sliced button mushrooms	3oz
2oz	50g	butter	¼ cup
1oz	25g	flour	1oz
½pt	275ml	milk	1¼ cups
4oz	100g	home-smoked cheese, grated	4oz
		salt and pepper	
		pinch of cayenne pepper	
4	4	eggs, separated	4
1	1	egg white	1

Prepare a 7in/175mm soufflé dish, and heat the oven to 375°F/190°C/Gas 5. In a saucepan, sauté the mushrooms in 1oz/25g of the butter until soft. Remove with a slotted spoon and drain on soft paper. Add the remaining butter to the saucepan and melt it. Stir in the flour and cook together for 2 minutes. Gradually add the milk, beating to make a smooth mixture. Stir until it boils, then remove from the heat and beat hard until the mixture leaves the sides of the pan. Turn into a bowl and stir in the grated cheese, mushrooms and seasoning. Beat the egg yolks until liquid, then beat them into the flavoured sauce a little at a time. Whisk the 5 egg whites together until stiff enough to hold soft peaks. Fold them into the soufflé with a metal spoon. Turn gently into the prepared dish and bake for 30 – 35 minutes. Serve immediately.

PARTY DISHES

Smoked mackerel dip

8oz	225g	smoked mackerel, skinned and free from bone	½lb
4oz	100g	cottage cheese	½ cup
6fl oz	175g	single (light) cream	¾ cup
4tsp	20ml	lemon juice	4tsp
4oz	100g	margarine, melted	½ cup
		pinch each of grated nutmeg and cayenne pepper	
		salt and pepper	

Process all the ingredients in an electric blender until smooth. Add extra cream for a more liquid dip. For a lower-calorie one, substitute natural yoghurt for the cream.

Serve the dip chilled, with vegetable or pastry dunkers.

Smoked mackerel pâté *Serves 8 – 10*

2	2	hot-smoked or smoke-cooked mackerel, 1½lb/675g each	2
		salt and black pepper	
4oz	100g	softened unsalted butter	½ cup
2tbsp	30ml	double (heavy) cream	2tbsp
2tbsp	30ml	lemon juice	2 tbsp
		a good pinch of grated nutmeg	
		cayenne pepper	
		skinned, chopped pistachio nuts (optional)	

Remove heads, skin and bones from the fish. Break the flesh up roughly with a fork, and season. Put in a food processor with half the butter, and process briefly. Then add, in order, with the motor running, the remaining butter, cream (little by little), lemon juice and seasonings.

Turn the pâté into a jar, knocking on the table-top while filling to knock out air-holes. Cover with clingfilm or clarified butter, and refrigerate until needed. Use within 36 hours.

If you prefer, turn half the pâté into a glass dish, then sprinkle with a layer of chopped pistachio nuts. Top with the remaining pâté, and garnish with a ring of nuts around the edge.

Smoked trout mousse *Serves 4 – 6*

2oz	50g	onion, sliced	2oz
1	1	celery stalk, sliced	1
1	1	bay leaf	1
3	3	black peppercorns	3
½pt	275ml	milk	1¼ cups
1oz	25g	butter	⅛ cup
1oz	25g	flour	¼ cup
8oz	225g	finely flaked smoked trout	½lb
2	2	finely chopped hard-boiled (hard-cooked) eggs	2
		grated rind and juice of ½ lemon	
		salt and pepper	
¼pt	150ml	soured cream	½ cup + 2tbsp
2tsp	10ml	gelatine	2tsp
2tbsp	30ml	water	2tbsp
1	1	egg white	1
		chopped parsley	

Put the onion, celery, bay leaf, peppercorns and milk in a saucepan. Bring slowly to the boil, remove from the heat and leave to stand for 10 minutes. Strain. Melt the butter in a clean pan, stir in the flour and cook together, stirring for 2 minutes. Gradually stir in the milk, bring slowly to the boil and cook for 2 minutes, still stirring constantly to make a thick sauce. Take off the heat, and stir in the flaked fish, eggs, lemon rind and juice. Season well. Cool to tepid, then fold in the soured cream.

While cooling, soften the gelatine in the water in a heatproof jug. Stand the jug in very hot water and stir until the gelatine dissolves. Add a little fish mixture, then stir back into the main mixture. Cool almost to setting point. Just before the mousse sets, whisk the egg white stiffly and fold it in evenly.

Turn the mousse into a decorative bowl or individual dessert glasses. Chill. When set, sprinkle with chopped parsley.

Smoked salmon party flan *Serves 10*

		shortcrust pastry made with 8oz/ 225g/2 cups flour	
8oz	225g	smoked salmon, cut in thin slices	8oz
8oz	225g	cooked leaf spinach, drained	8oz
3	3	eggs, beaten	3
¼pt	150ml	milk	½ cup + 2tbsp
¼pt	150ml	single (light) cream	½ cup + 2 tbsp
		freshly ground black pepper	
		pinch of grated nutmeg	
1tbsp	15ml	Parmesan cheese	1tbsp

Use the pastry to line the base and sides of a 10in/250mm flan case or ring. Chill for 15 minutes. Lay the smoked-salmon slices evenly all over the base and sides of the flan. Cover with the spinach. Mix together the eggs, milk, cream and seasonings, and pour over the spinach. Sprinkle with the cheese. Bake the flan at 400°F/200°C/ Gas 6 for 25 – 30 minutes until set. Serve hot or cold.

Neat's tongue (crumbed smoked tongue) (1792)

3½lb approx	1.5kg	whole pickled, smoked ox-tongue (beef tongue)	3½lb
1	1	egg yolk	1
16 – 20	16 – 20	whole cloves	16 – 20
		dry toast crumbs as needed	
		melted butter for basting	

Cut out any bones, gristle or membranes at the root end of the tongue. Soak it in fresh water for about 4 hours. If heavily smoked, the tongue may need longer soaking and cooking. Put into fresh water in a heavy pan which will just hold it. Bring to the boil. Skim. Reduce the heat and simmer the tongue for 30 minutes per lb/450g and 30 minutes over, or as needed. Check the water level occasionally and top up with boiling water if needed.

Remove the tongue when tender. Strip the skin off without spoiling the shape. Beat the egg yolk until liquid, and brush the tongue with egg all over. Cover the tongue with the crumbs, pressing them on lightly. With a skewer, make small holes in a decorative pattern on the top of the tongue and insert a clove in each. Sprinkle the tongue with melted butter. Lay the tongue flat, garnished side up, on a flat dish. Bake at 375°F/190°C/Gas 5 for 20 – 30 minutes until the crumb and egg coating is set.

Serve hot or cold. Slice at the table.

Macaroni and smoked beef salad *Serves 4*

8oz	225g	Pre-cooked elbow-cut macaroni	8oz
4oz	100g	cooked green peas	4oz
½	½	1lb/450g can pineapple cubes in natural juice	½
3oz	75g	smoked beef	3oz
¼pt	150ml	French dressing	½ cup + 2 tbsp
1tsp	5ml	French mustard	1tsp

Rinse the macaroni under cold water, and toss in a cloth to dry. Turn into a bowl, and mix in the peas. Drain the pineapple cubes, reserving the juice. Chop the cubes and mix with the macaroni. Cut the smoked beef into small strips and add them to the salad.

Mix together the French dressing and mustard. Sweeten with juice from pineapple can. Toss salad with dressing.

Party choucroute garni *Serves 12*

4½lb	2kg	canned sauerkraut	4½lb
3	3	large onions, chopped	3
2 – 3oz	50 – 75g	lard	¼ – ⅓ cup
2tsp	10ml	caraway seeds tied in muslin	2tsp
½pt	275ml	white wine	1¼ cups
3	3	small tart apples, peeled, cored and sliced	3
1tbsp	15ml	sugar	1tbsp
		chicken stock (1pt/550ml/2½ cups)	
		salt and ground black pepper	
¼pt	150ml	Jenever (Hollands gin)	½ cup + 2tbsp
12	12	large smoke-cooked pork sausages (about 2oz/50g each)	12
12	12	smoked rindless bacon rashers (slices)	12
12	12	smoked pork hamburgers	12

In a large flameproof casserole, sauté the onions gently in most of the fat. When tender and golden, mix in the sauerkraut. Add the seeds, wine, apples and a little stock. The sauerkraut must not swim in liquid. Season to taste. Cover the pan and simmer for about 20 minutes, stirring occasionally. Season to taste. Add more stock as required. After 20 minutes, stir in the Jenever and top the sauerkraut with the meats. Cover and cook (15 – 20 minutes).

Serve with made mustard, chutney and crusty French bread chunks after any winter get-together such as carol-singing.

American smoked turkey salad *Serves 8*

8oz	225g	hot-smoked or smoke-cooked turkey meat without skin	1 cup
4oz	100g	home-smoked cheese	4oz
2	2	cold boiled potatoes, skinned	2
2	2	stalks celery, sliced	2
8oz	225g	cooked green peas	½ cup
12	12	apricot halves canned in natural juice, drained and diced	12
2	2	small shredded lettuce hearts	2
2tbsp	30ml	chopped chives	2tbsp
		salt and ground black pepper	
		juice of a lemon	
		a few drops of oil	

Cut the turkey meat, cheese and potatoes into ½in/1cm dice, and mix them in a bowl with the celery, peas, apricots, lettuce and chives. Season well. Dress with lemon juice and a few drops of oil shortly before serving.

Smoked chicken or turkey niçoise *Serves 12*

4 – 6tbsp	60 – 90ml	French dressing	4 – 6tbsp
1	1	small clove garlic	1
2	2	cans anchovy fillets 1¾oz/49g each, drained	2
		large leaves of 1 round lettuce	
6	6	medium tomatoes, skinned and cut into eighths	6
1	1	large green pepper, seeded and shredded	1
1	1	small onion, cut in paper-thin rings	1
1lb	450g	cooked, sliced green beans	1lb
1lb	450g	smoked chicken or turkey meat, cut in small thin strips	1lb
6	6	hard-boiled (hard-cooked) eggs cut into eighths	6
2tsp	10ml	dried oregano or basil leaves	2tsp
12	12	black olives, halved and stoned	12
		salt and ground black pepper	

Make a well-seasoned French dressing. Chop the garlic clove very finely and add it to the dressing. Halve the anchovy fillets lengthways and keep aside. Separate the lettuce leaves and use to line one or two large flat platters. In a bowl, mix together the tomatoes, pepper, onion, beans, meat, eggs, oregano or basil, and half the olives. Season well. Toss lightly with enough dressing to moisten.

Pile in a fairly flat layer on the lettuce leaves. Arrange the anchovy fillets in a lattice pattern on top, and garnish with the reserved olives.

Fruited smoked duckling *Serves 8*

8tbsp	120ml	seedless raisins	8tbsp
8fl oz	225ml	orange juice	1 cup
1	1	10oz/285g can apricot halves in natural juice (8 halves)	1
2	2	smoked ducklings salt and ground black pepper	2
3tbsp	45ml	French dressing watercress sprigs	3tbsp

Soak the raisins for 4 – 6 hours in the orange juice. Drain them, reserving the leftover juice. Carve off the whole breasts and legs of the ducklings to yield 8 handsome serving portions. (Use the remaining meat for a smoked duck risotto or pie.) Arrange the portions on a flat platter. Drain the apricots and season the cut sides lightly. Fill each with 6 – 8 raisins and arrange between the duck portions. Sprinkle each duck portion with about 1tbsp/15ml of the reserved orange juice and 1tsp/5ml of French dressing.

Serve with a brown-rice salad made with 1½oz/35g dry rice per person.

Smoked egg and cheese party salad *Serves 8*

1lb	450g	shredded and coarsely grated raw vegetables (cabbage, lettuce, carrot, green and red pepper, celery)	1lb
4oz	100g	grated smoked cheese	4oz
2oz	50g	sultanas (golden raisins)	2oz
6	6	smoked eggs mayonnaise	6
½tsp	2.5ml	smoked sea-salt pinch of cayenne pepper	½tsp
¼ bunch	¼ bunch	watercress leaves, chopped	¼ bunch

Toss together the salad vegetables, cheese and sultanas. Chop 2 eggs coarsely, and mix them into the salad. Bind with enough mayonnaise to moisten but not hide the salad shreds. Season.

Pile up the salad on a flat plate. Halve the remaining eggs lengthways and arrange in a circle around the base of the pile.

Smoker-party meat-platter with salad 'cigars' *Serves 12*

24	24	assorted smoked sausages	24
12	12	'mock' bacon rashers (slices)	12
12	12	chicken drumsticks or smoked burgers	12
3tbsp	45ml	French mustard	3tbsp
3tbsp	45ml	tomato paste	3tbsp
2	2	round lettuces	2
6	6	large firm tomatoes	6
½	½	cucumber	½
12	12	red radishes	12
12	12	spring onions	12
2oz	50g	smoked cheese	¼ cup
12	12	long soft dinner rolls	12
¼pt	150ml	mayonnaise	½ cup + 2tbsp
		meat glaze (canned consommé, simmered until syrupy)	

Use two or three different types of sausages, either home-smoked or purchased. Arrange all the meats on a large platter which can also hold the rolls, and the piles of salad. Mix the mustard and tomato paste and place a generous dab on each burger. Keep aside any left over.

Wash and shred lettuce, and slice thinly the tomatoes, unpeeled cucumber, radishes and onions. Flake the cheese. Split the rolls. Mix any remaining mustard and tomato mixture with the mayonnaise and spread some of it over the cut sides of the rolls. Fill the rolls with a few shreds of lettuce and the other salad ingredients; do not fill too full.

Reshape the rolls. Warm the glaze until just liquid and brush over the rolls to make them glossy dark brown. If you wish, fasten a strip of gold paper round each as a cigar band (use a strip cut off a birthday-cake band).

Arrange the rolls on the platter with the meats. Use the remaining salad ingredients and mayonnaise mixture to garnish the dish, separately or mixed.

19
Rules for Safe Smoking

Any operation using fire and heat carries some risks. Equally obviously, raw meat or fish that is not properly handled can become tainted and perhaps dangerous to eat. Possibly, some scientists say, people who eat large quantities of certain heavily smoked foods may be more liable to get cancer than others.

But any risks – and the remedies – are easy to pinpoint. If you always follow a few simple rules, smoking food and eating it is as safe as cooking and eating any other kind of food.

AVOIDING FIRE HAZARDS

A home-built smoke-house or kiln for cold smoking often gets its smoke from a wood fire built outside the structure, either on the ground or in a shallow pit (see page 36) from which a covered trench carries smoke into the smoking-chamber. A home-made or impromptu hot-smoking 'oven' nearly always has an open wood fire to produce the heat and smoke needed, while a portable smoking-box is usually fuelled by methylated spirit lighted in pans underneath it. In all these cases, any risk that the flames may spread is easily avoided simply by using commonsense. Before starting to smoke, make sure that the fire or fuel-pans are well clear of any long grass, bracken or bushes, and that no drooping branches overhang the site. Clear away loose dry leaves and grass, or bits of paper. If the fire or fuel-pans are on turf, sprinkle it thickly with sand or gravel; trim away dry turf or grass from the edges of a pit. Prevent any sudden gusts of wind from fanning the flames by erecting an adequate windbreak.

Take special care when using any impromptu smoking apparatus. It is possible, for instance, to build a shelter of woven green branches to smoke small fish in at the riverside, but – apart from leaking smoke – it always carries the risk that the branches are dryer than you think and catch fire. A small commercially made 'hot-box' used indoors over spirit-filled pans *must* be placed on a stainless-steel work-top or in a flagged fire place; no draughts must fan the flames and it must not be within reach of a fluttering curtain or any other hazards. Remember that methylated spirit rises as it heats, and may spill over the top of a full pan and run burning over uneven ground. Make sure that any appliance heated by spirit fuel stands on a flat *and* level surface, and that the fuel container is never filled to the brim.

Keep a bag of sand or cinders and a small fire blanket with your smoking equipment, just in case flying sparks or spilt liquid spirit set grass or other inflammable material alight.

FOOD HYGIENE

Any food you smoke should come from a reliable supplier or be caught in unpolluted water. Be particularly careful if you live in a warm or tropical climate, or where your fish comes from the Pacific Ocean or the Mediterranean. Dangerous bacteria are more rampant, and the risk of getting meat which has not been properly slaughtered or fully matured, or shellfish which is unfit to eat, is a real possibility. The US Food Regulations governing the supply and processing of smoked foods are an excellent guide to procedure for anyone living in southern Europe or other warmer climates, or where food supplies are less strictly regulated than in Britain or the United States.

Never forget the need for scrupulous hygiene when preparing any food for smoking. Whether you are working in your own kitchen or on a picnic site, make sure your knives are clean, bright and sharp. Give the same cleaning care to the mincer (grinder) used for sausage-making, and to skewers, hanging hooks and other equipment. Always use clean foil or a scrubbed board to process food on, and have clean hands. Don't think that a scrap of dirt will not matter because the food has been brined, or will be smoked: you could be wrong.

The length of time you leave food in brine or cold smoke is your personal choice (see Chapter 12). But remember that the brining and smoking times suggested in this book are not intended to give you food for long storage. As for smoke-cooked food, always treat it as smoke-flavoured fresh food – it must be refrigerated and eaten quickly. The really dangerous bacteria which might be lurking in food which has not been processed or chilled enough do their work unseen – often without any telltale odour.

If a food has not achieved the weight loss recommended when you think it should have, don't kid yourself that it must have been processed long enough because the colour is fine and it was smoked as long as usual. When you store any cold-smoked food, don't omit to label it because you are in a hurry or think you will remember how it was processed and by which day it should be used. A week later you will have forgotten.

When you smoke-cook any food, follow a standard recipe and allow enough time and fuel to cook it thoroughly. Do not skimp because you have almost, but not quite, enough methylated spirit left, or because people are clamouring to eat. If you refrigerate it before eating it, don't take chances: it is easy to think 'That's been smoked, it'll keep another day, so we'll eat the fresh meat (or fish) first'. That day can slip into being two or three, long enough for the smoked delicacy to become distinctly unattractive if not perilous to eat.

If you use any of the modern variations of smoking-plus-cooking, the main thing to remember is that food must never be allowed to cool slowly in air and then be re-warmed mildly. That gives bacteria the breeding-bed they like best. If the food is destined for a hot meal, cool it if you must – but do so as quickly as possible, over ice or chilled water, or wrapped in wet cold paper. Always reheat it to a high temperature.

Above all, remember that no amount of processing will make food fresh and delicious if it is already stale and tainted. Smoking will not mask off-flavours or poor quality, or tenderise tough meat, though it will improve the flavour of dull tasteless food. Foods for smoking can be cheap, but they must be fresh and top-quality of their kind. The better the raw food, the better your smoked products.

IS THERE A CANCER RISK?

A good deal of modern research into the possible risk of getting cancer from eating smoked foods has been done in Germany and Hungary, where most people eat much more smoked fish and sausage than elsewhere in Europe or the USA. One special group of people in West Hungary have been studied in particular because they eat almost no fresh meat, only home-smoked products, and have done so for generations. For their smoking, they use mostly aromatic resinous softwoods such as juniper.

Scientists' findings show that these people do get cancer, especially stomach cancer, more often than other Hungarians. The same is true of some Icelandic fishermen who eat mostly smoked fish.

The main culprit seems to be an aromatic hydrocarbon in smoke called benzo(a)pyrene or BaP for short. The experts have therefore tried to find a 'safe' level of BaP in smoked food, below which there is little or no risk of getting cancer. On the present evidence they reckon that a level of 1 microgram per kg in smoked foods is a practical and reasonably safe level to aim at.

Meats and sausages, fish and cheese have been studied; hot smoked and cold smoked, industrially smoked and home-smoked foods, and sausages and fish with and without skins have been compared. The BaP level varies, but none of these foods hits a dangerously high level *when smoked over hardwoods*. The story is quite different when they are smoked as the West Hungarians smoke them – over resinous softwoods. The average BaP content of home-smoked meat, bacon, ham and sausages then shoots up; sausages for instance gain 0.83 micrograms of BaP per kg.

The obvious main way to avoid any possible danger of stomach cancer from eating a lot of smoked foods is simply to stick to hardwoods as smoking fuels.

Our varied modern diet also protects most of us. Only a few pockets of people in rural or coastal Germany, Iceland and Eastern Europe now live almost entirely on smoked meats and sausages or heavily smoked fish. However keen you may become on home smoking, you are unlikely to want to eat only smoked foods. The BaP level in your body can only creep up very slowly – so slowly that you will die of old age before your smoked food can do you any harm!

Suppliers

Innes Walker Ltd
56–58 Queen Elizabeth Avenue
Hillington Industrial Estate
Glasgow G52
(Electrically-assisted smokers)

Weber-Stephens Products (UK) Ltd
Tricorn House
Hagley Road
Birmingham B16 8TP
('Kettle' smoke-cookers)

Brooks Productions Ltd
88 Windsor Road
Southport
Merseyside PR9 9BY
(Hot-box smoke-cookers,
cold-smoking attachments)

Frank Odell Ltd
70 High Street
Teddington
Middlesex TW11 8JE
('Kettle'-style smoke-cookers)

Living Flair Ltd
103 Brunel Road
Earlstrees Industrial Estate
Corby
Northants
('Kettle'-style smoke-cookers,
wood-burning herbs and spices)

McConnell Salmon Ltd
Bloomsbury House
74 – 77 Great Russell Street
London WC1B 3DF
(Salmon for smoking)

Pinney's Smokehouses Ltd
Brydekirk
Annan
Dumffrieshire
Scotland
(Smoked foods)

British Meat
5 St John's Square
London EC1M 4DE
(Charts of meat cuts, etc)

John West Foods Ltd
54 Stanley Street
Liverpool 1
L69 1AG
(Canned fish and fruit)

McCormicks Foods Ltd
Patterson Jenkins PLC
Castle House
71 – 75 Desborough Road
High Wycombe
Buckinghamshire
HP12 2HS
(Dried herbs and spices)

Index